City of Lions

JÓZEF WITTLIN (born 1896) was a major Polish poet, novelist, essayist and translator. He studied in Vienna, where he met Joseph Roth and Rainer Maria Rilke, before serving in the Austro-Hungarian army in the First World War. He published one novel and numerous collections of poetry, many of which were characterised by their strong pacifist sentiments. With the outbreak of WWII he fled to France and then to New York, where he died in 1976.

PHILIPPE SANDS is a professor of Law at University College London. He specialises in International Law and International disputes. He has also published many books, including *East West Street* and *The Ratline*.

ANTONIA LLOYD-JONES is a prize-winning translator of Polish literature. She was awarded the Silver Medal for Merit to Culture by the Polish Ministry of Culture in 2019.

DIANA MATAR is a photographer whose work investigates issues of history, memory and state-sponsored violence. A graduate of the Royal College of Art, she has won many prizes and her work has been exhibited in institutions around the world.

EVA HOFFMAN is an award-winning academic and writer, whose books include *Lost in Translation*, *Exit Into History* and *After Such Knowledge*.

CITY OF LIONS

JÓZEF
WITTLIN

PHILIPPE
SANDS

Translated from the Polish by Antonia Lloyd-Jones
With photographs by Diana Matar

PUSHKIN PRESS

Pushkin Press
Somerset House, Strand
London WC2R 1LA

1 3 5 7 9 8 6 4 2

ISBN 13: 978-1-80533-001-1

Set in Monotype Baskerville by Tetragon, London
Printed and bound by Clays Ltd, Elcograf S.p.A.

www.pushkinpress.com

CONTENTS

PREFACE

Eva Hoffman

T HE PROTAGONIST of the richly interesting volume you have before you is not a person, but a place; and the texts and images included here are, in effect, acts of archaeological excavation and imaginative reconstruction. They bring alive for us a metropolis which was once seen as one of the grand cultural centres of Europe; but which, since World War II and the Cold War, has largely disappeared from Western consciousness behind an imaginative, as well as the real Iron Curtain.

Since the lifting of that great divide and the fall of the Berlin Wall, the great Eastern European cities—Prague, Budapest, Kraków—have become popular destinations for visitors from all over the world, and have been assimilated into our mental topography of Europe, and our understanding of a shared—for better or for worse—history. Lviv, later to emerge from the Soviet domain, still awaits such rediscovery; and there is no better place to start than with these two illuminating essays.

"My Lwów" and "My Lviv" were written over fifty years apart, and from very different perspectives; but both are pervaded by a sense of the city's almost magnetic fascination—and of great loss. Józef Wittlin spent his formative years in Lviv, but his brilliant and beguiling essay (here brought to us in its first English translation) was published in New York in 1946, just as the long years of his transplanted American existence were beginning; and it can take pride of place in that literature of exile which, in the terrible twentieth century, has produced so many masterpieces: *Native Realm* by Czesław Miłosz, Nabokov's *Speak, Memory*, or Brodsky's essays in *A Room and a Half*. Like many of these better-known works, Wittlin's essay has the lyricism and the density of detail which are the marks of nostalgic—although never sentimental—recollection.

The city evoked in these reminiscences brims with the sensuality of lush hills and the beauty of grand architecture; with nooks of intimacy and madeleines of local tastes; and with the kind of vitality, brio and charm which, in the interwar period, were often associated with the region of Central Europe known as Galicia. Can one analyse the ingredients of something as elusive as a cultural sensibility? Wittlin's Lviv was an entirely multicultural metropolis, long before such a concept arrived in our Western climes; a city where, despite tensions and conflicts—as well as occasional outbreaks of political violence—various religions and ethnic groups mingled with each other in street and café with ease and a kind of camaraderie; and where other kinds of borders were perhaps also more fluid and permeable than in the capitals of the West: boundaries between the (relatively) rich and poor, between the scamp and the upstanding citizen, between high culture and low, between vigorous earthiness and elegant stylishness. The one trait which seems to cut across all these distinctions and which marks, in Wittlin's account, a true Lvovian, is a deep suspicion of solemnity, pretension and all pomp. Interestingly, this is also what Milan Kundera, writing in a more analytic vein, identifies as the crucial ingredient which gave that part of the world its distinct sensibility and flavour. "Central Europe", in his essay entitled "The Tragedy of Central Europe", "has its own vision of the world, a vision based on a deep distrust of history. History, that goddess of Hegel and Marx, that incarnation of reason... that is the history of conquerors. The people of Central Europe... represent the wrong side of this history; they are its victims and outsiders. It's this disabused view of history that is the source of their culture, of their wisdom, of the 'nonserious spirit' that mocks grandeur and glory."

If the sceptical spirit was the essence of Central European sensibility, and intolerance of pomp the soul of Lvov, then Wittlin embodies both in his writing, and in the pervasive ironic wit he brings to everything he observes—including himself. It is a style which incarnates the very sensibility he is describing, and which is wonderfully rendered in Antonia Lloyd-Jones' lively and exact translation: rapier-sharp but never caustic, wistful but never sombre, whimsically anecdotal but never frivolous—not least because the awareness of the coming cataclysm pervades the essay, in allusions which are seemingly marginal, but all the more poignant for that. Wittlin was, of course, perfectly aware that, in pushing horror to the margins, he was "playing at idylls"; but here he asserts, so to speak, the privileges of exilic memory, and his right to remember, in the fresh aftermath of destruction, the textures, atmosphere and human variety of a world he had loved and lost.

The consciousness of that cataclysm, and the depredations of both the Nazi and the Soviet era, is central to Philippe Sands' moving chronicle of his journeys to the newly Ukrainian Lviv. His explorations partly follow in Wittlin's footsteps; but by the time he arrives, he finds a city which, within a recognizable physical topography, has been stripped of its former variety and, seemingly, of its memory. There are no traces of the ethnic or national melange described by Wittlin; and no markers commemorating sites of the genocide in which Sands' ancestral family was almost entirely exterminated. The sense of pensive melancholy pervading "My Lviv" derives from Sands' awareness of what is no longer there; and his quest is to penetrate the dark absences, and understand what was once within them. Diana Matar's beautiful black-and-white photographs reinforce the sense of pastness in the present, of a compelling darkness.

In his search for an unknown family past, Sands joins other second- and third-generation descendants of the Holocaust who visit remote sites of ancestral life and death, in a kind of symbolic reversal of exile. But he brings to his pursuit the unusual skills and the ethical perspective of an internationally known human rights lawyer—qualities which give his account a special interest and depth. His confrontations with the other "second generation"—the inheritors of the Nazi legacy—have the force of a moral drama, especially as he encounters the continuing, and reality-defying refusals to acknowledge Nazi crimes; and his determination to understand the truth, no matter how disturbing, is evident in his willingness to enter, through documents and records, the terrible mental world of Nazi perpetrators who were directly responsible for the extermination of Lviv's Jewish population, among whom Sands' own family were numbered.

The deletions and denials of memory Sands encounters are not only a Nazi but a Soviet legacy, bequeathed by a regime which enforced its Orwellian distortions of history with brutal measures. It is perhaps no wonder that so many Eastern European writers thought of memory as a moral force. And yet, the erasure wasn't complete, and Sands' difficult revelations are balanced by his affinity with and affection for the city, and the sense that something of Wittlin's

Lviv can still be found there—in its grand, if deteriorated buildings, its lively human encounters and intimate spaces, its cobblestone streets and its eccentric cafés.

But Sands' investigative instinct also leads him to a discovery which is as astonishing as it is reparative: the realization that the concepts of genocide and crimes against humanity, which are so crucial to his own work, were framed by two men—Rafael Lemkin and Hersch Lauterpacht— who lived in interwar Lviv for a while, and studied at the Lviv law faculty at the same time as his grandfather. It is possible, Sands intimates, that the powerful ethical principles developed by these professional ancestors also emerged from the cataclysm which had annihilated his family—that the legal conscience of these two Lvovians, nurtured at what was then a great university, was conjoined with an acute consciousness of atrocity and the urgent need to provide a stay against its most awful effects.

There are no easy conclusions to draw from the vicissitudes of a history as turbulent as shown in the *City of Lions*—as both Wittlin and Sands are well aware. The end of history seems to be nowhere in sight. But while the future of Ukraine is once again uncertain, "My Lwów" and "My Lviv" provide a synoptic vision and much needed insight into a city which was once central to Europe's civilization, and which is still—or once again—closely bound up with its future and fate.

JÓZEF WITTLIN

My Lwów

Translated by Antonia Lloyd-Jones

All this my heart remembers, saves and cherishes too,
The flavour of the bread there, and where the wild mint grew,
How joy would fill the soul there, flood it with heavenly bliss,
That land remains forever dear, the sacred memory persists.

LEONARD PODHORSKI-OKOŁÓW,
Patrimony

T HE TITLE OF THIS BRIEF account was imposed by the publishers, and absolves the author of the charge of using it to talk about himself. We might think nothing could be more pleasant than bathing in the warm waters of remembrance, or casting fond looks upon years gone by. This is an illusory state of bliss. For suddenly, from the bottom of our memory, monsters we would rather forget are bound to come floating to the surface of our consciousness. Another peril, a hundred times greater, that lies in wait for those who reminisce is the risk of self-admiration, because a weakness for the places where we spent our youth is often nothing more than love in disguise. It is not for Lwów that we yearn after all these years apart, but for ourselves in Lwów. Nor can there be any more dangerous falsifier of so-called reality than the memory. It falsifies everything: people, landscapes, events, and even climates. It is a known fact, for instance, that in the summer season in Zakopane it rains most of the time. And yet our nostalgic memory depicts the Zakopane summer in the full glory of sunshine, or in the late afternoon, pink-and-purple glister of the Tatras. We only remember Zakopane's bright days, just as we only remember the virtues of our dear departed friends. Thus we should also regard each image of the world that is stamped on our memory as reality—the reality of our soul. And then it won't actually matter if Lwów really was as we recollect it here, or different.

I can hear the voices of a thousand shades. I can hear the laughter of shades: people both dead and alive, but now so far away that they merely cast a shadow on our memory. There are many shapes that I no longer recognize. They have blurred in my memory, merged with others into an amorphous, though picturesque mass, from which, through layer upon layer of time gone by, the pungent scent of white lilac gushes out and chases me all the way here. Some insistent noises call to me too, such as the rasp of a tram turning the corner from Ruska Street—by the Wallachian Church—into Podwale ["Below the Ramparts"]. This chaotic throng of crippled memories, phantom memories, pushes its way under my pen like a crowd of displaced persons flocking to an UNRRA[1] soup kitchen. Each spectre from the past is homeless, hungry and frozen to the bone, until it is taken in and warmed up with a word of compassion. But even then it won't be back in the right place yet.

So here I am, summoning up the ghost of Lwów past, for a sort of "Forefathers' Eve"[2] in miniature. Don't be afraid of this ghost. We're going to celebrate our "Forefathers' Eve" in a jolly way, as it wouldn't be right to commemorate a city of good cheer the way it is seen, heard and all but physically handled nowadays by nostalgia.

II

My Lwów! Mine, although I wasn't born there at all. After some precise calculation I can say that I spent a total of eighteen years in Lwów. Not so very much for a man who, rightly or not, is regarded as a Lvovian and takes pride in the fact. In truth, they were the years of my boyhood and early adulthood, and thus decisive for the whole of my later life. And most probably, if not for the so-called Great War, though small compared with the latest one, today I'd have been sitting on Hetman Embankment, or the Governor's Ramparts as yet another old penny pincher, yet another retired schoolmaster from one of the Royal-Imperial gymnasiums where the lectures are given in Polish. I'd have received polite bows from balding, grizzled gentlemen whom I had once sent to stand in the corner as a punishment; but I'd have been the first to bow to my former female pupils, or even to kiss the hands of those solemn matrons. Or I'd have fed pretzels (their crisp glaze crusted with salt) to the now non-existent goldfish in the malarial pond, drained long ago, at the bottom of Kiliński Park.[3] Even Lwów's cobblers never called this park by that name, as nowadays it is simply Stryjski Park. Or I'd have gone for a walk each morning, on an empty stomach, bareheaded, come rain or shine, whatever the season—along the paths around the High Castle, above fabulously wooded ravines, as a real live member of the "Idiots' Club". I'd also have gone to ogle the frilly skirts and listen to the Royal-Imperial military music in the Jesuit Garden. The official name of this old, enchanted park at the very heart of the city is *Pojezuicki*—literally "Post-Jesuit". In days of yore, before the Voltairean edicts of Emperor Joseph II, it was the domain of the Society of Jesus. But show me a Lvovian who could spit out such a complicated name! "Where are you going?" "To the Post-Jesuit Garden!" I'm sorry, but even Mayor Ciuchciński[4] himself would never have had the gall to talk like that. Likewise, the relatively new name of the same garden, "Tadeusz Kościuszko Park", would never have crossed the lips of anyone in Lwów. Not that the Lvovians had anything against the Commander-in-Chief, but from an innate abhorrence of solemnity, which is so well loved in other parts of Poland.

From time to time I would go off to watch the younger generation playing a friendly sport known as *kiczki*,[5] which flourishes in the sleazier suburbs. In my young day this game was played with particular passion on the slopes of Hycel Hill, known for show as the "Hill of the Execution of Teofil Wiśniowski and Józef Kapuściński".[6] The mere fact that honourable memorial sites were known by one set of more familiar names in the everyday life of Lwów, and by another set in the tourist guides, testifies to the above-mentioned dislike of all manner of pomp. Anyone who took himself and his own doings too seriously among us was called a ceremonial ass. And so if not for the "great" war and its consequences, I'd have gone on sitting to the end of my so-called earthly journey on one of the municipal benches of the royal capital city of Lwów. For some Lvovians make this journey in a sitting position—not necessarily all in one go—in Brygidki Prison.

Where are you now, park benches of Lwów, blackened with age and rain, coarse and cracked like the bark of medieval olive trees? Generations of penknives have etched girlfriends' names on you, now perhaps the last reminders of old crones buried in Janowski or Łyczakowski cemetery. Where are you today? Who, and in what language, is now carving their lovers' initials on you? Or maybe in one of the many harsh wartime winters you were stolen away for firewood, and in the flames that consumed you, all those people's hearts hissed their last? Let's not slobber over the benches, because we'll soon find that it's not them we're drooling over, but ourselves.

I left Lwów in the autumn of 1922. In other words, "my Lwów" was mainly the Lwów of the Austrian partition era, the capital of the "Kingdom of Galicia and Lodomeria and the Grand Duchy of Kraków with the Duchies of Auschwitz and Zator". What? That's right—Auschwitz. (Nowadays, everything goes black before my eyes at the mention of that name.) Next, "my Lwów" was the Polish-Ukrainian war of 1918–19, and the first, still bleeding years of regained independence. Later on, I went back there at least once a year for a happy visit. And I'd go with a pounding heart (inasmuch as I have such a thing at all), like an old-style bridegroom to his wedding. I would watch impatiently for the suburban woods to appear in the carriage window, and then for the towers to jump out of the undulating greenery, one after another, so dear to my heart (inasmuch as I have one), of St George's, St Elizabeth's, the Town Hall, the Cathedral, the Korniakt and the Bernardine. And the cupola of the Dominican Church, and the cupola of the City Theatre, and the Union of Lublin Mound, and the bald Piaskowa ["Sandy"] Hill. (During the German occupation the sands of this hill soaked up the blood of thousands of martyrs.) I was rarely conscious, as the train decelerated and triumphantly drove into one of the twin entrance halls, clinging together like Siamese sisters—one of those semicircular, harmoniously vaulted glass halls of the Main Station. Now, on this tiring voyage known as life, I have pulled in at many a station, but none of them, except perhaps for the Gare du Nord in Paris, has ever prompted such excitement in me, such "metaphysical shivers", as the late Stanisław Ignacy Witkiewicz[7] would have said. The Main Station was the pride of every Lvovian. I have a perfect memory of it being built at the beginning of our beloved twentieth century.

As a small tot I used to go in the company of my so-called *bonne* to inspect the work involved in erecting this miracle of engineering and architecture, which was to eclipse even the Racławice Panorama[8] itself. And so it did. For in all contemporary Galicia and Lodomeria with the Grand etcetera, there was no other building as richly and brilliantly illuminated. In later years the Main Station served me many a time as a refuge from mathematics and physics. We are plainly refugees throughout our lives: from cradle to grave we are always running away from something. In those days I was just bunking off school, or to put it a more Lvovian way, I was "going *hinter*". I would take the ŁD tram[9] from Łyczaków to Gródek and, instead of getting a second-rate mark in class at the Royal-Imperial VII gymnasium on Sokół Street, I would spend a very pleasant morning in the smart second-class waiting room. It wasn't a waiting room—it was a veritable drawing room, full of candelabras, mirrors, gilding, and soft sofas and couches upholstered in fragrant leather. On top of that, it carried a scent of the world far away, the magic of foreign lands. One waited here not only for one's train to depart, but as if for happiness itself, to which the station clerks did not sell tickets in those days. The first-class waiting room was not accessible to mortals below the rank of Your Excellency or Baczewski.[10] And so, in the second-class waiting room, under a guardian, life-size portrait of Archduke Karl Ludwig wearing a fair beard and the parade uniform of an officer of Uhlans, I used to read so-called Sherlocks; in other words periodical editions of the masterpieces of detective fiction. One obtained this "unwholesome reading matter", as my parents and tutors called it, either through barter among friends, or from the true Castalian Springs of all kinds of literature in Lwów, in other words the second-hand bookshops of Bodek the Father and Bodek the Son, Menkes the Father and Menkes the Son, and also the Igels, Father, Son and Grandson. Ah, you fathers, sons and grandsons of the Lwów second-hand book dealers, proudly settled in your dynasties the entire length of the even-numbered side of Batory Street! What an inhuman death it was your fate to die in the infamous years of the massacre of the Polish Jews.

But let us go back to returning from "the world outside" to the Main Station, which apparently no longer exists. After 1922, a watershed year in my life, the relatively long journey from the station to Łyczaków was like a path of atonement for me. The whole length of this path I was nagged by self-reproach: how could I have moved away for ever from such a beautiful, friendly city? But whenever my one-horse cab finally turned into the home territory of Abbot Hoffman Street, my conscience would quieten down. I felt like a penitent, absolved of all sins thanks to the pilgrimage he has undergone. For on Abbot Hoffman Street I would be greeted by the caretakers of the various houses where I had once resided (No. 3, No. 6, No. 9, No. 20, No. 30 and the house on the corner, 2 Bonifratry Street), as well as those

where, as I live and breathe, I had never once set foot. The vestibules of all these "realties" smelled strongly of camphor, used by the caretakers who greeted me to polish the wooden stairwells to a shine. Despite their efforts, the smell of tomcats lingered heavily in the air there too. Allow me to continue to sentimentalize. So here to greet me on Abbot Hoffman Street and its cross streets—Bonifratry, Gołąb and Mikołaj Rej—were the locally resident legal clerks, copyists and solicitors, schoolmasters, advisers to the Railway Board, and also to the Treasury's General Counsel, retired senior advisers to the late Royal-Imperial Viceroyalty, consultants to the Provincial Authority, Magistracy clerks, chimney sweeps, Jewish second-hand traders and postmen, the great Ukrainian writer Mihailo Yatskiv, Szapowałek the cobbler, Engelkreis the publican, Genia Smoczek the harlot, Schwarz the grocer, or in Lvovian style, the *grajzlernik*,[11] Pafnucy Duma the *grajzlernik* and his lovely wife and equally lovely daughters. The white-haired lady grocer "Justianka", mother of the late Kazimierz Justian, a great star of the Warsaw stage, always used to ask me the same question: "What are they saying about my Kazio in Warsaw?" The poor woman outlived her beloved Kazio, and they had soon stopped talking about him in Warsaw.

Yes, yes, in Łyczaków the people of Łyczaków greeted me because I was a child of Łyczaków, even though I was born right on the border of Volhynia. Every return I made to the cobbled streets of Łyczaków was something like the return of the prodigal son. Though these people must surely have resented me for the fact that, while I could have been quietly schoolmastering away in Lwów, as fragrant as one big "garden of health", I preferred to go off to a dubious theatre in Łódź, which could be described as anything but fragrant. Maybe they had another grudge against me because instead of bringing joy to one of the comely (and how comely!) young ladies of Łyczaków, I had joined in matrimony with a "Congress Kingdom[12] girl". But who knows, perhaps at the bottom of those effusive greetings a seed of hope may have sprouted that I had finally thought it over, got it right, mended my ways, and would never leave Lwów again. But nobody ever tried to persuade me to divorce. Yes, I was a prodigal son of Lwów.

Get in line, you wayward memories! Stop breaking ranks, or I'll call a cop in a black oilcloth shako, with a metal crescent moon under his chin and a curved broadsword. I'll whistle, and a whole pack of those old boys will come flying up from the depths of time. First of all, officers with golden sabres, in black *Schlussrocke*[13] with gold buttons and gold epaulettes. All that glitters is not gold, but the fact is, these Royal-Imperial Polish *Schwarzgelberen*[14] looked very stylish, like naval officers. Outstanding among Lwów's police-officer elite was Captain Tauer; with his black curly moustache, he specialized in dispersing pre-election demonstrations. After him come the famous agents, or inspectors, or to put it plainly, narks. Though dressed in plain clothes, they wore bowler hats, Habig hats, or even top hats. They were led by the great Baziuk, "*the* Baziuk", the terror of the bandits and ne'er-do-wells. After him, some way behind, come: Przestrzelski, Janklewicz, Lieblich and Grinzberg, whose head was blown off, top hat and all, by a Ukrainian grenade in 1918. Inspector Grinzberg, who specialized in terrifying and searching female domestic servants, who in every good home were suspected of stealing the silver, the batiste lingerie, the Ihnatowicz soaps and other locally produced toiletries, had a beautiful daughter. The urban minstrels composed long and wistful ballads about these heroes of Lwów criminology, sung not only in the cells of the *furdygarnia*, meaning the police lock-up on Jachowicz Street, not only in the main prison, in other words Brygidki, and not only at the "on Batory" [Street] clink. The length and breadth of the Czerwień Towns region,[15] and wherever there was a nick or a decent boozer in the area, you could hear those ditties about whisker-faced Baziuk, scourge of the bold *dezenter*[16] Józiek Marynowski, or about the fight between the rozzers and Białoń the bandit. It is strange what a large space in this city's folklore is occupied by the police, the courts and the world of crime. For nowhere else perhaps were murders, safe-cracking, and even pettier, more pocket-sized transgressions wrapped in such romantic charm as in this singing capital of street urchins and senior advisers, who lived, though not all that well, from throwing the urchins in jail. The essence of being a Lvovian, which I am endeavouring to sketch in rough outline, is an extraordinary mixture of nobility and roguery, wisdom and imbecility, poetry and vulgarity. The flavour of Lwów and its culture is tart, reminding one of the taste of that unusual fruit that appears to ripen nowhere but in the Klepary suburb, and which is called *czerecha*—the wild cherry. Not quite the *wiśnia*, or common cherry, and not quite the *czereśnia*, or sweet cherry. But the *czerecha*. Nostalgia even likes to falsify flavours too, telling us to taste nothing but the sweetness of Lwów today. But I know people for whom Lwów was a cup of gall.

III

Just as the *gavroche* was once a typical specimen of Parisian human fauna, so the most common representative of Lwów's anthropoids is the street child, known to the entire civilized and uncivilized world by the Magyar name *batiar*. However, it would be a mistake to believe that every *batiar* is a child of the street, sired by the gutter. The *batiar* could be born in a patrician mansion or on a nobleman's estate. Quite a number of them went on to shake up the Viennese parliament, or go about in a professor's gown, rattling a dean's, or even a vice-chancellor's chain, rather than a pair of handcuffs. And to jabber in Latin—well, all right, with an Upper Łyczaków or a Zamarstynów accent, but that couldn't possibly offend the ancient Romans since we don't really know how spoken Latin sounded. Anyone who knew the late Professor Wilhelm Bruchnalski, one of the most brilliant experts in Polish studies at Lwów University, or the late Professor Zygmunt Łempicki, whose reward from the Germans for the many years he spent teaching their language and literature at Warsaw University was death in Auschwitz, will not accuse me of exaggerating. And while we're on the subject of the martyrs of this war, we should also pay tribute to another highly Lvovian individual, not unlike the *batiar*, and that is the late Professor Kazimierz Bartel, a great "somebody", scholar, statesman and patriot. There's a good deal of the *batiar* in the city itself, in its entire physical and moral structure. Elevations and depressions, exaltation and mundanity, balmy odours and the stink of the River Pełtew.[17] The purest Italian Renaissance, both church and secular, the works of Paweł the Roman and Pietro Italo-Krasowski, the equally rich baroque, and alongside it the Viennese Secession and some vulgar trash. The *batiar*-city is unpredictable. You never know when it will jump from pathos to the grotesque, from heroism to playing the goat, from a funeral with three pairs of Kurkowski's horses dyed black, to the mythical "veterans' ball" that ended at midnight with the appearance of two civilians who didn't say a word to anyone, but just put out the lights and smashed everyone in the kisser.[18]

As well as the *batiar*, another famous type was the Lvovian *kołtun*. Like everything Lvovian, it is complex and difficult to define. For what does the word *kołtun* mean? Literally it is an ailment of the hair, caused by dirt. In Latin, *plica polonica*. Metaphorically it is an unenlightened person, uncouth and backward. We would be wronging Lwów's average *kołtun* with this definition. Because our *kołtun* is first of all a member of the "Strzelnica"[19] marksmen's fraternity. It's true that most of its members were not highly proficient in the humanities, being master craftsmen and senior representatives of various guilds, not excluding the butchers', but besides them the "Strzelnica" also included educated, refined people, and even, as we shall see, some scholars. On the whole, the Lvovian *kołtun* was a good-natured boor, an unsophisticated petty bourgeois, the hero of plays by Gabriela Zapolska.[20] With that a patriot, chiefly a local one, with a touch of overzealous flag-waving. At moments of pathos the *kołtun* was inclined to make great sacrifices—of somebody else's life and property. Sometimes even his own. Within my memory a major role was played at Lwów's Town Hall by the shooting-range *kołtuny*, who provided the city with several excellent mayors, such as the farrier Michał Michalski, the tinsmith Stanisław Ciuchciński and the printer Józef Neumann. It goes without saying that the "Strzelnica" held the majority among the city councillors. Each year the fraternal marksmen elected their king and, despite what we have said about Lwów's dislike of pomp, they would appear at the ceremonies in extremely lavish costumes, sporting *kontusze* (sixteenth-century noblemen's robes) and *karabeli* (sabres), like the armigerous aristocracy. This costume had long since been the privilege of Lwów's patrician class, and a sort of official uniform for mayors and deputy-mayors of the city, regardless of their origin and faith. One of the three deputy-mayors was always a Jew, who also donned a black robe and buckled on a sabre for gala occasions. Nobody was surprised, and nobody was shocked.

Of all specimens of the marksmen-*kołtun* clan the one that has stuck best in my memory is Councillor Walery Włodzimirski. By profession a chemist, his laboratory was on the ground floor of an old house on Jagiellońska Street, opposite the "Champagne Pavilion". I used to walk to school that way, and many a time I yielded to the temptation to peep inside through the low windows. To this day, I associate what I saw with alchemy rather than chemistry. It was just like Faust's workshop—an enormous hall, whether vaulted I no longer remember—crammed with tables, cabinets and shelves, on which a dense collection of fantastically shaped glass objects glistened. Bizarrely twisted tubes, funnels, communicating vessels, retorts and test tubes, empty or full of liquid in all sorts of colours. And in the mysterious depths there were stoves and ovens emitting smoke, bellows puffing away, all of it in unearthly, tawny gaslight. Sometimes incredible flames would belch forth and bounce off the batteries of glass over and over again. Clouds of steam would conceal the whole lot for a moment, and then once more reveal all this sorcery, in the midst of which a single human figure would be buzzing about—small in height, wearing a frock coat, with a ruddy face adorned with large, black imperial sideburns. He would often put a long glass pipe to his lips, prompting you to say: he's going to play a magical *dumka* to wake up the poisons sleeping in the jars and release the imprisoned deaths, which will start to writhe like snakes, charmed by the playing of a dervish. But I cannot remember any sound ever coming from his siphon, although Włodzimirski the wizard would keep ardently blowing, until his cheeks were bulging, and his black sideburns were spread wide like the wings of a great, exotic bird. Any minute now they're going to break free of his face and fly into the air. At such moments I equated Włodzimirski with Fregolo the sorcerer, who, next door at the "Dreamland" cinema, to the sounds of a harmonium, would leap out of fabulously coloured flowers onto the screen and disappear in a phosphoric cloud of smoke. That was one of the mirages of this poetic phase in cinematography, which was still young at the time. Yes, Councillor Walery Włodzimirski was undoubtedly the Lvovian Faust. And the fact that he often appeared in public in a black kalpak hat with a feather in it, and a *kontusz* with a *karabela* and a big gilded cockerel on his breast, also lent him a resemblance to the legendary Polish sorcerer, Pan Twardowski. Especially the cockerel. The spell was shattered one fine day, when I was told to deliver to Włodzimirski a small bottle wrapped in paper, containing a somewhat personal liquid. For why conceal it any longer? Our Faust did tests for almost all the patients in this part of town, until the pharmacists started doing it, or as they were called in centuries gone by, the "aromataries".

While we're on the topic of pharmacies, let us mention the ones that not only contributed to the good health of the Lvovians, but also to the aesthetic quality of the local landscape. Almost every one of them had its own patron, beautifully displayed on their shop signs. The choice of patronage over these arsenals of health often testified to the great imagination of the doctors of pharmacy, who, for some unknown reason, are said to lack it. If, for instance, the pharmacy at the junction of Zielona Street and Wincenty Pol Street entrusted its concoctions and its customers to the care of the Virgin Mary, that's fine. It wasn't just in Lwów that people prayed to Her for good health. Nor is there any need to explain the names of the "Holy Spirit" or the "Divine Providence" pharmacies (this one's signboard showed an enormous eye in a triangle). But why exactly did "aromatary" Antoni Ehrbar choose the Roman Emperor Titus as the patron of his pharmacy in lower Łyczaków, opposite the Church of the Sisters of St Clare? Surely not to spite the Jews, for whom that emperor was the destroyer of Jerusalem? His oval portrait was visible on either side of the pharmacy entrance in colourful medallions painted on glass, on top of which the entrance itself was crowned with a bust of the emperor made of imitation bronze, or plaster painted to look like bronze. To leave no room for doubt, we could read in three different languages that this was the pharmacy of "the Roman Emperor Titus"—*Zum römischen Kaiser Titus—Sous*[21] (!) *l'Empereur Titus* (!). Why on earth the French had to have their language crippled in Łyczaków it is hard to fathom; in my day there were not many resident Frenchmen, not just in Łyczaków, but in the whole of Lwów. There were in fact a few native "Parisiennes" to educate the children in the so-called better homes, but half of them were born on the River Pełtew rather than on the Seine; bearing in mind that the consul of the Third Republic himself, a fine-looking gentleman with a white patriarchal beard, was a Pole by the name of Żebrowski. He was an "honorary" consul, of course, because Lwów did not maintain diplomatic relations with any that were not honourable.[22]

A highly popular pharmacy, among the healthy as well as the sick, was the "Hungarian Crown" on Bernardyński Square. The name requires no commentary, since, as the saying goes, "Pole and Hungarian nephews be" (but whose?). This beautiful pharmacy belonged to town councillor and "Strzelnica" member Dr Jan Piepes-Poratyński. Over the years, the name Piepes, an embarrassing leftover from his goodly grandfather, who wasn't a Poratyński at all, was lost by the wayside, and he became just plain Poratyński, an impressive man with a large, black, altogether splendid beard. He looked particularly majestic in his *kontusz* at the Corpus Christi procession alongside the long-and-grey-bearded, but modestly sized "Saint Tulia", as everyone called the famously pious Vice-Chancellor of the Polytechnic and town councillor Maksymilian Thullie. But the "Hungarian Crown" pharmacy was renowned not so much for the virtues and charm of its owner as for the most beautiful shop window in all Galicia and Lodomeria with the Grand etcetera. It was so lovely that no pharmacy goods were ever displayed behind it. The windowpane itself was on display. On this sheet of glass of tremendous proportions, worth three hundred crowns—not just Hungarian, but Austro-Hungarian crowns (I can tell that I'm gradually starting to think in American categories)—and so, on this three-hundred-crown super-window, etched in matt tones by the use of special acids, there was an exquisite crown of St Stephen, the patron saint of Hungary; there was also a wide variety of Secession water lilies and garlands, all of which paid tribute to the tastes prevalent at the beginning of our beloved century. One time when some vandals broke this—luckily—insured masterpiece of the glazier's art, all "civilized" Lwów was deeply affected, and the newspapers covered the story in as much detail as many years later they would write about the beautiful Gorgonowa[23] who, at the heart of the Brzuchowice district, killed her stepdaughter, Lusia Zarembianka.

The pharmacy and the crime story are generally rather discrete concepts, but not on Bernardyński Square. For it is only a few steps from (Piepes) Poratyński's pharmacy to the Criminal Court and the adjoining prison. One has merely to walk across the square and head in the direction of a small well with a naked, winged nymph. So let us ponder awhile the special feature of Lwów that were the so-called sensations, or killings, or alternatively, murders. That was a fine era, when once or twice a year someone in our city sent somebody else to their eternal rest. For the Christian denominations, the main site for eternal rest was Łyczakowski cemetery. The local preference was to murder either members of one's own family, or of other families. But there was also the occasional murder of a would-be member of one's own family, not out of hatred for them, but quite the opposite. These victims paid the price in blood for a refusal or inability to be joined by blood ties with the killer. An incident of this very kind was handed down to posterity on the wings of a song about Lewicki. (One of those genuine, Pacyków Lewickis.)[24] For love of a married actress, he murdered her. I cannot remember the whole song any more, but there are still scraps of it running, or rather dancing, through my head to the tune of "Away, troika!", which deserve to be quoted, e.g.:

> *Lewicki, see what love can do,*
> *Your lover's corpse lies in the tomb,*
> *The gallows is awaiting you,*
> *The hangman's rope shall be your doom.*

or:

> *Had you not lovèd another's wife,*
> *Now you surely would be free,*
> *You'd not be at the end of life,*
> *But fit and well to high degree.* *

Anyone who winces at my fondness for Lvovian *batiar*-criminal songs should deign to recall that in the early years of our beloved century—at the gymnasium on Sokół Street—I had the honour of being a pupil of the late Adam Zagórski, Poland's greatest expert on the literature and music of this genre. So anyone who reproaches me for taking pleasure in nothing but imponderables, for overrating trivialities and for disregarding respectable tradition, history, geography and architecture, in short, the culture of *Leopolis semper fidelis*, and for not saying a word about Lwów as the "intensifier of the Polish spirit", or about "threefold" Lwów—as it was called by the excellent mayor it had in the seventeenth century, who was also a fairly good poet (though not as good as his brother Szymon), Józef Bartłomiej Ozimek, known as Zimorowicz—anyone who might think badly of me for appearing to turn a blind eye to "The Oath of Jan Kazimierz",[25] the Ossolineum [Institute

---

* I made up the final verse myself because I have forgotten how it goes in the original, and even the eminent Lvovian and eminent painter Zygmunt Menkes was unable to remind me of it.

and Library], the Colosseum [Theatre], the Dzieduszycki [Natural History] Museum, the [Prince] Lubomirski [Art Museum], the Stauropegic Monastery and the Racławice Panorama, in the first place is wrong, and in the second I can assure him, to paraphrase Terence, that: *Leopoliensis sum et nihil leopoliensis a me alienum puto.* But I will admit that for my childish sensibilities the arrival of Buffalo Bill's circus (in 1905, if my memory is not deceiving me), or the hanging of Czabak the murderer are just as epic events as the arrival of Emperor Franz Joseph, the assassination of the Viceroy, Count Andrzej Potocki, or the time eggs were thrown at his successor, Michał Bobrzyński. This occurred during Juliusz Kleiner's doctoral graduation ceremony, which happened *sub auspiciis Imperatoris.*[26]

As it is the most amusing of these events, let us recall the visit graciously paid to Lwów by the aged monarch in the year 1903, on the occasion of "imperial manoeuvres" in the Szczerzec area. At the time, the aforementioned Mayor Ciuchciński was already making his mark. Clothed in the glory of his office, he was sitting beside His Royal-Imperial Apostolic Majesty himself, in the plush "imperial" box at the City Theatre for a performance of *Aida,* or perhaps *The Haunted Manor.* This rather unusual circumstance was making him feel a little awkward. (Who wouldn't?) All the more since His Royal-Imperial Highness was benignly praising the Lwów opera. Moved by this acclaim emanating from the highest lips in the land, Ciuchciński gibbered the immortal words: "*Jawohl, Majestät! Die Sänger sind gut, nur die Choren sind schlecht.*"[27]

Honi soit qui mal y pense!

IV

Unlike Wilno and Kraków, Lwów has no legend to do with its birth. There were no Mendogs or Gedymins[28] to change its nappy. No wolves lulled it to sleep with their mythological howling. It is true that the city's emblem is a lion. Its entire name is made up of lions too, and—to some extent—so is its personality. Its mane and its terrible roar, which on Judgement Day or when an atom bomb falls only the deaf will hear, remind us of the trademark of the Metro-Goldwyn-Mayer film studio. But it is not a legendary lion. It is the purely historical emblem of the town founded in the thirteenth century by Prince Halicki—whose first name was Lew [Leo I of Galicia]. Nor did Lwów have any princesses who drowned in the style of Kraków's Wanda[29]—maybe because it has no river. In fact, older people and geographers maintain that Lwów is on the Pełtew River. But who has ever seen it? By the time of my generation we could not see it; at most we could smell it, for in a couple of spots on the northern outskirts of the city, beyond the High Castle and at the point where the "Babi" Mill once rattled away, the Pełtew attempts to emerge from under the earth in which the municipality had it buried. Apparently in olden times it flowed down the very middle of today's Hetman Embankment, but it was so foul-smelling, and so shallow, that not only would no patriotically-motivated princess, but not even a personally-motivated common skivvy would risk jumping into its dubious waters. So within our fathers' memory the poor Pełtew was filled in and demoted to the role of a canal. Now it weeps underground, but it keeps flowing, and does so right underneath the City Theatre, just like its Parisian cousin, the Bièvre brook, which is also buried alive, rolling along beneath the Opera building. There is an interesting kinship, and also an outward similarity between these two theatres, located in the two cities in the world closest to my heart—inasmuch as I possess one.

All right, so Lwów hasn't got a decent river, or a legend. What would it need a river for? The urban planners and tourists say that if Lwów were graced with a river, it would be a second Florence. In my view Lwów has more greenery than Florence, though less of the Renaissance. Moreover, it resembles Rome, for like Rome it is picturesquely spread over hills, and there are four wells murmuring away in the Marketplace, above which stand the very fine statues of Diana, Amphitrite, Neptune and Adonis. Lwów also has its Santa Trinità dei Monti—it is the Carmelite Church, which also has high steps leading to it. As for the impoverishment of the landscape for lack of a river, there are not many cities in the world that are equally interesting in terms of hydrography. At the gymnasium on Sokół Street

I was taught that in so-called Kortumówka, where there used to be a shooting range (not the *kołtun* one, but for the Austrian infantry), a strange phenomenon occurs. There is a small but extremely significant cottage there. For whenever it pours with rain, a pair of gutters at one corner of the cottage guide the water into a creek, which flows into a brook, which flows into a stream, which flows into the River Bug, which flows into the Vistula, which flows into the Baltic Sea. Meanwhile, the rain flowing from the gutters at the other end of the cottage by a similar route supplies the River Dniester, which flows into the Black Sea. By this means Lwów is at one and the same time on the Black Sea and the Baltic. So why should it need a river?

The name "Kortumówka" does not say much nowadays; at one time it said more. It came from Ernest Kortum, the first owner of these wooded hills and the small manor house, below which the watershed runs by. This Kortum arrived in Lwów immediately after the third partition of Poland, as an eager servant of the Austrian Emperor Francis I, having formerly been an eager servant at the court of King Stanisław August. These things happen, and they're not worth discussing. We're talking about Kortum because he is remembered for hating the Poles and hating the Jews. And as is often true of people who hate people, he loved the noble ideals of humanity. Thus he played an eminent role in the history of Lwów's Freemasons, as the co-founder, with another German called Fessler, of the "Zum Biedermann" lodge. In the final years of the Republic and in the ones that followed, Lwów was swarming with apron-wearing brothers, grouped within lodges such as "The Three Goddesses", "True Friendship", "Perfect Equality", and so on.

I first heard about the existence of Masonic lodges in my early youth. I was highly impressed by the costume and insignia of the Grand Master of the old Polish Freemasons, exhibited in a display case at the Prince Lubomirski Museum—they made almost as great an impression on me as the wings and armour of a Hussar from the Battle of Vienna. I knew how the Hussars spent their time—beating up pagans. But what sort of masons these were, what they built and where they did their building work, and why they sat in *loges* did not cease to intrigue me, even in more mature years. The Polish word for a lodge—*loże*—also means a loge, or box at the theatre; they could be imperial, mayoral, to one side, over the stage or at the National Casino... No masons had been seen there since the construction work was finished. And if one of them ever made a trip to the theatre as a spectator, he usually bought himself a ticket up in the gods. Whereas "the gentlemen", who went to the premieres and sat in the loges, were more likely to don tail coats than aprons. How very mysterious it all seemed. I looked for those apron-wearers' loges on every single level of the new City Theatre, the old Skarbek Theatre, at the Jewish Gimpel Theatre and the Ukrainian Taras Shevchenko Theatre. To no avail. But I did notice that in some of Lwów's social circles they whispered about Masonic lo(d)ges as something scandalous. And in an age when we were particularly sensitive to things that were whispered, I imagined that it was simply to do with the loges at the small variety theatres which were strictly out of bounds to me, or at the sort of café known as a *tingel*—the Zehngut at the Hotel Bristol, and chez Franz Moszkowicz at the Casino de Paris. There, by night, lascivious orgies were held with the participation of socialists, nihilists and the naked soul of Stanisław Przybyszewski.[30] *Apage, Satanas!*

But anyone who believed in God could pray to their heart's content in Lwów. For as well as the Klepary cherry tree and the watershed in Kortumówka, a third singular feature of our city was that it had no fewer than three cathedrals. Three cathedrals: Latin, Greek-Uniate and Armenian. Each magnificent for a different reason, each erected in a different style, in a different century. The favourite here is undoubtedly the youngest: the Greek Catholic Metropolitan Church of St George, which is also remarkable for the fact that it was built in the eighteenth century not by an Italian, but by a Pole, who happened to be the commandant of Kamieniec Podolski. In fact he did not have a very Polish name—it was Jan de Witte. What sort of a commandant of Kamieniec Podolski he was it is now hard to determine, but anyone who has seen his two creations in Lwów—the Dominican Church and St George's Cathedral—will agree that he was a pretty good architect. De Witte managed to choose a very lovely hill for his Cathedral, and he knew how to harmonize the rococo architecture with nature and the open air. This St George's is colossal, castle-like, fortress-like, and at the same time light and graceful, almost ethereal. It hovers over our city, and it hovers over our youth like a celestial wedding ship, especially delightful in spring, when it rises above the lush greenery of the parks and the blossom-speckled orchards, which wind around the lower storeys of the Cathedral on gentle slopes. Imbued with all the aromas of Lwów's generous primavera, this temple soars towards the clouds like a symbol of heavenly triumph over the torments of earthly existence. In its gloomy interior the famous Ukrainian choirs sing Akathist hymns at the gilded "Tsar's Gates". And even the human voices here are the gilded, Byzantine kind. The deep, dark bass tones seem to float up from the very bottom of this yawning well, where every human soul settles accounts with its own sins. From the bottom of the well whence Yohanan cried out before death who he was and whose coming he heralded. And right beside it, on the grass, on the Cathedral Hill, horses graze merrily. I thought they were the reserve chargers of St George himself, patron of the Cathedral, feeding on the grassy shoots of the urban pasture, but I was mistaken. They were from the Archbishop's stable, the carriage team of His Excellency Metropolitan Szeptycki, grandson of Aleksander Fredro.[31]

The first time I ever stood at the entrance to the Vatican, I was reminded of St George's in Lwów. I would not wish to offend the Apostolic Capital, but the reader will already have guessed which I liked the better.

We are not writing a Baedeker guide, but we cannot fail to mention the Latin Cathedral, a bizarre creature in terms of both style and shape. Basically Gothic, in the eighteenth century this building succumbed to the baroque. In those days this was the site of the flourishing "Metropolitan factory" of Archbishop Wacław Hieronim Sierakowski, who for years on end employed masses of local and foreign architects, sculptors, painters, "marblers" and "mosaicists", until he had given the Cathedral the look it has today. Inside, distinct by token of its moderation and harmony, there is a purely Renaissance chapel housing the tombs of the Kampian brothers, Paweł and Marcin. Both of them were doctors, and Marcin was also Ciuchciński's predecessor at the Town Hall. The Kampian brothers were envied their posthumous splendours by two other seventeenth-century sibling-citizens—another doctor of medicine, Dziurdzio[32] (Jerzy) and Paweł Boim, as the name "Dziurdzio" bears witness, Wallachians by origin. And for their eternal rest they built an even grander mausoleum in the immediate vicinity of the Cathedral. It is hard to describe the staggering richness of this "Gethsemane Chapel", so named after the main bas-relief, above the altar, depicting Christ in the Garden of Gethsemane. The "Boim family chapel" is simply dripping with stone-carved people, angels and saints, inlays and mouldings, and not just on the inside, because the entire façade looks like a black layer cake made of stone as well, or a maharaja's jewel box. It is the work of German artists. Yet anyone willing to strain his neck will not regret the effort, because a look at the inside of the cupola and the lantern tower really will remind him of Florence and of majolica ware by the della Robbias.

I was somewhat afraid of the Boim chapel at the age when phobias take shape in us. In those days it included a very smart mortuary with tail-coated corpses in open coffins. But one time I went in there on purpose, to see the poet Adam Dobrowolski, who had died of consumption. The anthologies of that era include a passionate poem of his entitled *Evviva vita!* The author of this paean to life lived no more than thirty years.

It would now be fitting to say a word or two about the Armenian Cathedral, but I prefer to keep my mouth shut, in fear of a man who knows every inch of it by heart, and who is now living and teaching in Washington. He painted the famous murals in the Armenian Cathedral, and his name is Professor Jan Henryk de Rosen.

So let us be lulled instead by the memory of the Bernardine Church, by the vision of its unforgettable silhouette against the Lvovian sky, which nostalgia has cleared of clouds for us. The massive façade is crowned by an architrave with triglyphs and metopes, which carries prominent moulding, and also supports a wonder of grace and rhythm: a high baroque frieze. By each volute on either side of the triangular frieze stands a stone monk, as if on watch. The effect of these monks, especially against a clear sky when the moon is full, is truly unparalleled. High in front of the church, on a column, the double pedestal of which is decorated with stone rococo lanterns, kneels St John of Dukla, with his arms outstretched. Below him sway chestnut trees in full bloom. The pink and white flowers stick up like bunches of candles, lit for the saint's prayer, a prayer for the salvation of Lwów. Next to it, behind the monastery wall, there is a fragrant orchard. Yet another orchard in the middle of the city. Birds twitter in the branches, and from the far side of the orchard, from Wałowa Street, I can hear the noise of hundreds of voices. It's the long break at the Bernardine branch of our gymnasium. There's a bell ringing, but not in the church. It's the old janitor Bazyli ringing the school bell, the break is at an end, our youth is at an end, and there's peace and quiet at the Bernardines and on Wałowa Street. The only place where they're missing is inside us.

The Bernardine Church could be regarded as the most beautiful in Lwów if it did not have some half a dozen rivals. In the nearby vicinity stands the classically Renaissance Church of the Dormition of the Mother of God, also known as the Wallachian—because it owes its charming existence to the generosity of the Wallachian *hospodar* Miron

Mohyła,[33] who hid from the Turks in Lwów. A tall tower adjoins the church, regarded as the prettiest to have been erected in the Renaissance style on Polish and Ruthenian lands. It was endowed by a Cretan Greek called Korniak or Korniakt [Constantine Corniactos]. Ringing out from it is Lwów's mightiest bell, the Kiryło. And hiding bashfully in the courtyard of the Stauropegic Institute we find the annexe to the Wallachian Church—the Chapel of the Three Kings, aristocratically austere, with a truly Florentine loggia. In its customary manner, Lwów prefers to call this chapel the Bałabanowska, from the surname of the donor, Balaban, who was also Greek.

Balabans, Korniakts, Mohyłas, Boims, Kampians— what sort of a motley crew is this? That's Lwów for you. Diversified, variegated, as dazzling as an oriental carpet. Greeks, Armenians, Italians, Saracens and Germans are all Lvovians, alongside the Polish, Ruthenian and Jewish natives, and they are Lvovian "through and through". But why is there a winged lion looking down so challengingly from above the gate of No. 14 on the Marketplace? It has set up home right opposite the Town Hall, and is bothering the two lions that guard the entrance to the municipality. Surely the reason why it looks so proud is that the small municipal lions are illiterate—they're ignorant *kołtuny*, while he is an educated lion. For he is resting on a large open book, in which it says: "PAX TIBI MARCE EVANGELISTA MEUS".

("Peace to you, Mark, my evangelist!") What is this? From this lion and from this Latin there waft a combined odour of stagnant water, honeymoons, fish, cuttlefish, wine, olive oil and wisteria—and in the Lwów Marketplace we can hear the strokes of oars against gentle waves growing louder and louder. We can hear a long whistle—it's the *vaporetti* putting in at swaying pontoon-stops, clouds of doves beating their wings in thunderous applause to Ferdynand Feldman in the role of Shylock and landing on the roof of the Procuratie. "Ah, go down to the gondolas!"[34]

Whence this Venice on the interred Pełtew? How on earth did St Mark's lion end up here? The Republic sent it in days of yore, along with its trade representative, and placed it above the gateway to Massari's house. These efforts were evidently profitable, as in former times Lwów was a more important foreign trade centre than in our day, when Professor Henryk Grossman devised the Eastern Fair[35] on Powystawowy Square.

I could mention many more of Lwów's stone curiosities, such as the Golden Rose Synagogue on Blacharska Street. Once I was even encouraged to write a play about the "Gildene Rojze", who in quite Shakespearean circumstances saved the Renaissance synagogue from demolition.[36] And what lover of art could casually walk down Żółkiewska Street without entering the old Orthodox Church of St Paraskeva? And without examining its great seventeenth-century iconostasis, featuring seventy paintings in Byzantine

style? By the so-called deacon's door there were *praznichki*, or pictures, handed to the congregation to kiss on holy days... O God! God of the Poles, the Ukrainians, the Armenians, God of the Lwów Jews, totally and utterly annihilated! I could go on endlessly about all the sanctuaries that were so lavishly raised to You in this city, but time is pressing me on towards more worldly matters. The candles are burning down in all the churches and temples, the night is getting darker, and soon at the "Strzelnica" the spirits of all the roosters that adorned the breasts of Lwów's kings of marksmanship will start to crow.

Of kings! Kings! The royal capital city of Lwów knew other kings, not just the marksmen. Kazimierz the Great was extremely fond of this town, rebuilt it after it burned down and bestowed many privileges on it. Queen Jadwiga gave the city a diploma in which we read that "to no citizen, either within the city, or without the city, shall any violence or injury be done, and everyone, Ruthenians, Armenians, Saracens and also Jews shall be protected by its laws". On 1 April 1656 King Jan Kazimierz took his memorable vow at the Latin Cathedral. And if we happen to wonder about the Lvovian fondness for kissing small hands, or at least to say *Całuję rączki*—"I kiss your little hands"—then who knows, perhaps the genesis of this custom should be sought in the year 1658, when the Sejm granted envoys of Lwów's bourgeoisie not just the privilege of voting at their assemblies, but also of kissing the royal hand.

But now let's be done with kissing and with kings, or I'll be accused of royalist sympathies, though in fact I only remember one king in Lwów: Wasiński, king of the housebreakers. I never kissed his hand.

Far more important than kings in our city were the mayors. We have already mentioned Zimorowicz, and Ciuchciński too, yet we also had mayors who were men of a totally different calibre, a kind that fully justifies the presence of the lion on the city's seal. Men such as Marcin Grozwajer. In 1648 he played the same role as the mayor of Warsaw, Stefan Starzyński,[37] but with greater success. In other words, he commanded the defence of Lwów when it was threatened by Khmelnitsky's Cossacks and by Tugay Bey's Tatars. Grozwajer himself writes that Khmelnitsky demanded "that we hand over all Jews, as those who are the cause of this war". As we can see, the cause of all wars and every kind of evil in the world did not change from Khmelnitsky to Hitler. Grozwajer continues: "We gave the response that we could not hand over the Jews for two reasons—first that they were not our subjects, but those of the royal Republic, and second that they bore the same costs and hardships as us, being prepared to die along with us and for us." In the eighteenth century another mayor, Marcin Solski, refused to recognize the Austrian Partition. He sent a memorandum to the first imperial governor of Lwów, Count Pergen, and to General Count Hadik in which he proved (after Emil Kipa,[38] I quote Solski's *ipsissima verba*):

"that the city of Lwów cannot swear an oath to the new authority, since it has sworn one to His Majesty the Polish King". In 1914, when the Russians captured Lwów, and the shooting-club mayor Neumann fled to Vienna, the whole burden of responsibility and care for the city was taken on by the handsome, grey-bearded deputy-mayor, Dr Tadeusz Rutowski. He took advantage of his own mild deafness whenever he didn't want to listen to things he didn't want to hear. And so on leaving Lwów, the Russians deported him to the depths of the Tsarist Empire as a hostage. And shortly before his death, when he returned to Lwów, he was the object of universal idolization. Yes, we had more than just *kołtuny* at the Town Hall, guarded by *kołtun* lions.

V

Before we pass from Lwów's stone fauna to creatures of flesh and blood, let us devote a warm word or two to the people of stone and bronze who have served many a loving couple as a "rendezvous sycamore".[39] For reasons of age and rank, we should give priority to Jan Sobieski on Hetman Embankment, all the more since he is our city's only stone cavalier. A red-blooded steed, grazed by a royal spur, rears on its hind hooves, supported by its mighty tail touching the plinth, on which a Turkish cannon lies in pieces. This battle charger is heroically lunging towards the Galician Savings Bank. The victor of the Battle of Vienna himself bears a remarkable resemblance (especially for the Ukrainian) to Bohdan Khmelnitsky. Waving a mace, he's pointing out the enemy to his invisible troops, who should be imagined in the rear, in the aptly named "Viennese" café. Sobieski's monument has rarely provided patronage for devotees of Cupid. Instead, swarms of worshippers of a different divinity have been drawn to it—of Mercury, who here, in the open air, under the linden and chestnut trees, had one of the numerous branches of his temple, i.e. the Black Market. But not far away, on Mariacki Square, Apollo reigned supreme. On a high pedestal, at the foot of a soaring pink column, Mickiewicz has come to a modest stop. A wide pilgrim's mantle traditionally covers his slender shoulders. His head is bare. Nobody has ever seen Mickiewicz in a hat. A winged, fine-looking, half-undressed woman has flown down from the roof of Sprecher's house and, having attached herself to the column in mid-flight, is handing the astonished bard the ancient instrument on which neither he, nor any other man of letters has ever played, but which even people with higher education mistakenly call a lyre. Mickiewicz's monument was not suitable for amorous encounters either. Whereas it was the favourite rallying point for all manner of demonstration. Patriotic processions usually disbanded here after listening to fiery speeches. In the background, behind the column, on the roof of the house where Dittmar & Co's oil-lamp store was located—as soon as dusk began to fall—the city's first electrically powered advertisement

would come on and go off, come on and go off: for the Bajka ["Fairytale"] cinema. On and off, on and off, the large light bulbs arranged in the shape of the letters B, A, J, K and A, formed a luminous accompaniment to the cadences of an orator as he assured the crowd in a mighty roar:

"Our influence is on a historical scale!"

"BAJKA," said the sign.

"If the Equine Casino[40] thinks it'll win election to the Sejm this time too, it is highly mistaken!"

"BAJKA!"

Here all the national and social-revolutionary anthems were sung, here on the day of the Romanovs' jubilee a portrait of Nicholas II was ceremonially burned. The next day His Excellency the Royal-Imperial Viceroy had to apologize to the Russian consul.

The statue of Agenor, Count Gołuchowski, at the corner of the Jesuit Garden and May the Third Street was more suited to lovers than to politicians and black marketeers. Some politicians simply hated it, occasionally giving vent to their loathing by chipping off an ear, or the nose, or some other easily detachable part of his body or attire from the author of the "October Diploma".[41] Opposite the Industrial Museum, on Hetman Embankment, Hetman Jabłonowski[42] stood in the bushes, inconspicuous but clad in armour. In the belief that the illustrious hetman would be better placed opposite the Jesuit Church, an enterprising municipality had him transferred, in the Polish era, to Trybunalski

Square. But that hetman had bad luck. One dark night some unknown pranksters stole him, leaving his empty plinth in the square. But what is our glorious police force for? In no time they managed to recover the knight, who was reinstated in Trybunalski Square, and as a consolation prize was gilded like a walnut on a Christmas tree. Our other statues worth mentioning include Franciszek Smolka[43] on Smolka Square. There he stood, as an indomitable symbol of parliamentarianism and democracy: with his back to the Equine Casino, where the Podolian and other counts spent their time ardently playing cards. The bourgeoisie devoted itself to the same thing at the City Casino on Akademicka Street. There, on a small square, stood the modest little bust of a count, writing lovely verses. All Poland used to sing, and perhaps still does sing the painful choral anthem to his words: *With the smoke of fires...* In my mind this bust, of Kornel Ujejski,[44] is associated with a whiff of loin chops, which were fried almost daily in the Casino kitchen for the members and their guests. Not far away, on a square named after him, sitting in an armchair, with goose quill in hand, was the greatest count in Polish drama.[45] There he sat, looking rather offended—probably by the actors, who were very good at playing chess at the Roma and Scottish cafés opposite, but when it came to his comedies at the City Theatre... oh well, let's not be too hard on the dead.

Yet Lwów didn't erect monuments to nobody but counts and poets. The cobbler Kiliński had his monument too, in

Stryjski Park, which no Lvovian dared to call Kiliński Park. The *sukmana*-clad hero of the Battle of Racławice also had one in Łyczakowski Park, known, in his honour of course, as Bartosz Głowacki[46] Park. But let's be done now with counts, heroes and poets made of bronze and stone. Someone'll think that in "my Lwów" there weren't any living people at all. But we did have live counts—hordes of them, no end of heroes and dozens of poets. The first living, breathing poet I ever met was on a very crowded train, known as a *Bummelzug*, carrying Sunday trippers from Brzuchowice to Lwów. Even in the corridor there was such a crush that I very nearly squashed a venerable old fellow with a white, but beautifully trimmed beard. He cast a benign eye on me, and began to interrogate me in a kindly way: what was my name, which school did I go to, what did I want to be in life, what was I reading, and so on. "He must be some sort of an inspector," I thought to myself, "Court Counsellor Court-ski, the devil knows." I was thirteen at the time, and I didn't trust benevolent old men who put indiscreet questions to youngsters. Suddenly the old boy asked point-blank: "And do you know who I am?" I had no idea. I fearfully shook my head.

"Haven't you learned my poetry by heart?"

I was stricken with panic: what if I had to recite something? But quick as blinking, my fear gave way to curiosity as to who he might be. I thought and thought—Maria Konopnicka![47]—flashed through my mind, for we owed most of the poems and so-called passages in our readers to that particular poet. But common sense warned me in time, and I refrained from saying her name out loud. After all, Maria Konopnicka was a woman, which this old gentleman was plainly not. So who was he? I thought and thought. At school, apart from Konopnicka we were not spared the interminable epic poems of Syrokomla.[48]

"Mr Syrokomla?" I blurted rapturously.

The old man clouded over. The warm, benevolent sparkle vanished from his Santa Claus eyes. Only his glasses went on glistening like ice.

"No!" he said sternly. "Guess!"

I felt as if I were falling into an abyss, drowning. As a last resort I clutched at the beard, the white trimmed beard and spectacles. I had seen them somewhere before: I had seen them in illustrated magazines, although the face was more oval. But it was him! It was definitely him!

"Mr Sienkiewicz?" I whispered in an otherworldly way.

The kindly old uncle had instantly metamorphosed into a terrible old granddad.

"What a shameful thing to say! Sienkiewicz does not write poetry. Do you know the poem, 'Who are you?'—'A little Pole!'?"[49]

I did, I did know it, and at once I reeled off the next line: "'What's your symbol?'—'The white eagle'." I was saved, although I still had no idea who the writer was. But he was placated now. His vanity, so quick to react even at such an advanced age, had now been satisfied. It never occurred to him that I might not know his name, as I knew his famous work by heart.

"Come and see me at the Ossolineum, my boy," he said, in a friendly tone again. "I'll give you a book!"

As soon as I got home I consulted my Polish readers and confirmed that I had had the honour of travelling from Brzuchowice with Władysław Bełza. I never went to see him at the Ossolineum.

That was my first encounter with a real live poet. Making the acquaintance of others was less embarrassing. For them, at least. Gradually I came to know almost every one of them who lived in Lwów, and thus: the blind poet Stanisław Barącz, collaborator on the literary journal *Chimera* and translator of *Faust*, and the eternally youthful Stanisław Maykowski, a scholar of Polish literature, who mass-produced poems that he read out to his countless female admirers at the Strzałkowska gymnasium, after which he tossed them (the poems, not the female admirers) into an enormous trunk or a sack, whence only a few made their way to the editorial offices of the local journals. I liked debating with the serious highlander Józef Jedlicz, who was a solid lyric poet and theatre reviewer. He did a very fine translation of *The Birds* by Aristophanes. Of course I knew Henryk Zbierzchowski, and to this day I regret the prank that I had the youthful temerity to play, which involved writing his obituary, and having it published in the

Poznań-based *Zdrój* ["Source"], when he was very much alive. The ageing Zbierzchowski answered me back with a caustic little verse in the satirical journal *Szczutek* ["Fillip"], which I found rather flattering. We are cruel when we're young. We're tough on derailed careers. We regard our jaded colleagues' failed ambitions, prematurely frustrated by the fight for existence, as a topic for mockery. And until life gives us a proper slap in the face we cannot begin to imagine how much sad resignation there is in a poet who, for so-called bread, and sometimes—as in this case—wine too, as well as other such beverages, is obliged to write rhymes every day of the week for *Gazeta Codzienna* ["Daily News"] or *Ikac* ["Illustrated Daily Courier"]. Zbierzchowski soon consigned my schoolboy joke to oblivion, and wrote about me very warmly in the same paper where he published his rhymes, which I had ridiculed in the obituary. Now he really is dead, and can no longer read these words, with which I bid him farewell and apologize to his exuberant, bohemian and very Lvovian soul.

Only once in Lwów did I see Leopold Staff, that Łyczaków-district Florentine from the era of Lorenzo the Magnificent. It was in 1912, as he bowed before the curtain at the City Theatre, called out at the premiere of his play *Laurels*. My dream of knowing him personally only came true many years later, in Warsaw. There too I met the now Varsovian, formerly Lvovian, writers Karol Irzykowski, Kornel Makuszyński and Feliks Przysiecki. In fact, before

the first war I used to see Przysiecki in Lwów almost every day, making his way to the editorial office of *Wiek Nowy* ["New Century"], which was next door to our school on Sokół Street. I had no inkling that this long-nosed dandy, this spindle-shanked reporter for Laskownicki's organ,[50] was one of Poland's most reliable lyric poets.

Yet the idol of my youth was a man from Kujawy who had settled in Lwów, Jan Kasprowicz. In 1920, when I shook his hand for the first time, I thought the ground was going to give way beneath me. And I was surprised that this stocky, pot-bellied man with the wrinkled, parchment-like face of a sad satyr, his forehead as domed as the cupola of the Dominican Church and bisected by a curl as black as soot, that this tubby Marchołt[51] with the Gothic eyebrows of Mephistopheles, from under which peered the eyes of a shepherd boy, did not thunder or roar like the Kiryło bell, or like the organ in the Cathedral. I was surprised that Kasprowicz was a human being at all, and emitted a human voice. Sometimes, when I came close to him, he gave me the impression of a walking mountain, one of the lesser Tatra peaks, and I thought I could hear the rush of a waterfall or tumbling scree. Kasprowicz was a live element, an avalanche on the cobblestones of Lwów and a walking myth, off to one of the cheap breakfast bars for a glass of wine. Where have those days gone, where are those places, in which even the characters of poets had such a magical effect on the young?

Of my literary contemporaries, the one closest to me was Jan Stur. A friend from the same school, in the class above, he deserves a more extensive memoir than I can devote to him here. An inspired poet, mystical, not always comprehensible, a haunted prophet, a true missionary, he wrote long epic poems, not just in Polish but in French and German too. We made our debuts at the same time in Poznań, and our first books came out on the very same day. Stur can be regarded as a successor to Przybyszewski, but also as a precursor of many of the poets who are fashionable nowadays. He spent a few years fighting heroically for what at the time was called new art, for expressionism and for Christian pacifism. He also wrote ardent essays, resurrecting Tadeusz Miciński and Sar Péladan.[52] He reduced naturalism and realism to a pulp, and castigated the cabaret offshoots of Warsaw's "Skamander"[53] group. He flickered like a noble flame, imprisoned in a small, ailing body, until he was snuffed out by tuberculosis, having survived for twenty-eight years. This death marked the end of my youth.

In the same year as Jan Stur, an opponent of his was buried at Łyczakowski cemetery, the slightly older, more restrained poet and journalist Jan Gella. These two men used to have heated arguments, and it very nearly came to a duel. A few years later they were followed to the graveyard by a third Jan—Zahradnik. A phenomenally talented lyric poet and the apple of Maykowski's eye, when he was still at school his poetry was being published in *Słowo Polskie*

["Polish Word"]. His sensitivity and maturity were quite simply suspect at such a young age: they did not portend a long life. And he misspent it, he drank—this favourite of the gods—and graduated to galloping consumption, having upset a number of writers with his venomous articles. I remember that sunrise in spring, when after an all-night drinking session I escorted Zahradnik, who was then a pupil in the seventh class, to the convent school run by the Congregation of the Resurrection Fathers on Piekarska Street. Strict discipline was applied to the pupils there. In drunken desperation I tried to bribe the doorkeeper monk not to report to his father superiors where and how student Zahradnik had spent the night. Poor Zahradnik!

Yes, gradually our entire memory becomes a cemetery. Wherever it takes you there are graves. The graves of those who died a "natural" death, ceremonially buried and loudly lamented. And now, like a terrible hump that has sprung up on the back of the memory, heaven knows who dug them or where, are the mass graves of victims of the most recent slaughter! Nobody wept over them. In 1939 the poet Stanisław Rogowski perished in Lwów. Later on the following poets and writers suffered a martyr's death: Halina Górska, Aleksander Dan, Tadeusz Holender, Józef Kretz-Mirski, Włodzimierz Jampolski and my pupil from the gymnasium, Karol Dresdner. Refusing to go into the ghetto, Henryk Balk took his own life. May the soil of

Lwów lie gently on them, if they were granted the mercy of lying in the ground.

A separate *ultimatum vale* is due to Ostap Ortwin. His real name was Katzenellenbogen, which made people laugh if they had a weak grasp of the German Middle Ages. Located on the Rhine, if it hasn't been bombed, is the fourteenth-century fortified castle of the Counts Katzenellenbogen. A Katzenellenbogen also shows up as a sponsor of the greatest German medieval lyric poet, Walther von der Vogelweide (1170–1230). Ostap Ortwin was not a count, but it would be hard to imagine a more aristocratic figure and soul. And as for the sponsorship of poets, he was right into it. He discovered Staff, and paved the way for Stanisław Brzozowski[54] to achieve fame, and especially understanding. He was a superb critic, but he didn't choose to write. And even if he did, he hadn't the time, because he never stopped reading. He read everything, from Spengler and Benda to the introductory articles in every daily journal. He was in the habit of expressing his opinions in a loud roar, which made the Café Roma's large windowpanes shake. That was where he mainly used to sit in his spare time from gainful employment. Before the first war he was an editor for Połoniecki's publishing houses, during the war he was an Austrian military judge, then a major in the Polish judicial corps, then an official at the Eastern Fair. He took each occupation seriously, and laughed at all of them, and at himself. Perhaps only the gods on Olympus knew how to laugh like he did. As the last president of the Lwów Writers Union, Ortwin seems to have been the only Polish writer of Jewish descent before whom the anti-Semitic blockheads shrank back with reverence. He seemed altogether inviolable. Tall, broad-shouldered and swarthy, with white hair, bushy eyebrows and a black Cossack moustache, his appearance alone was enough to halt the urges of lowlifes in their tracks. He chided the policemen who asked him to prove his identity for making loud threats against futurism late at night on the sleepy streets of Lwów. The scolded cops went on to salute him as if he were their most senior lord and master.

Ortwin had a doppelgänger who used to walk about Lwów, an engineer called Piotrowski. He even dressed the same way. Whenever the two lookalikes passed each other in the street, they doffed their ridiculous black hats with wide brims. Thus for many years they bowed to each other, although they were not acquainted at all. They were merely acknowledging their similarity and their awareness of being twins. In 1942 it turned out that Ortwin was not inviolable. The Germans drove the great, recalcitrant soul out of that "lordly" figure. If there are cafés in the afterworld, Ostap Ortwin is sure to be sitting in one of them right now, hunched over a pile of newspapers, that sacrificial pile on which he placed his own literary ambitions during his lifetime. And he is laughing out loud from behind the front page of *Czas* ["Time"], or rather "Timelessness", reading and reading non-stop, shouting, thundering, and laughing at us all, until the vault of heaven starts to shake.

VI

Let us come down from heaven to this earthly vale, since we're already on our way to the bar. There were plenty of them in Lwów, and each one exuded a different aura and attracted a different clientele. The general majority were cafés of the Viennese kind, where three glasses of cold water were served along with a small cup of coffee, places with more-or-less-alluring lady cashiers at the counter, who apportioned cloakroom tags, teaspoons and sugar to the waiters. The waiters and "Obers", or senior waiters who took the money, were usually recruited from among the German settlers, and were called Bechtloff or Bisanz. At any time of day you could walk into any one of the bigger cafés and call: "Mr Bisanz!", and a stocky fellow in a dinner jacket would be sure to come forward and politely respond: "At your service, Councillor (Count, Squire, Professor, Doctor)." "Mr Bisanz! The bill!" "Mr Ober! A mélange!" "Mr Bechtloff, a cappuccino!"—these are the echoes of bygone days.

There were cafés in Lwów that were only frequented by men. The appearance of a member of the fair sex in a place like the Europejska at the corner of Jagiellońska and May the Third Streets was a disturbing rarity, although in those days some ladies were already getting involved in business. Whereas other, more refined cafés were full of femininity of every possible shade, age and attire. The *odor feminae* gave these places a provocative, elite aspect and invited both daydreaming as well as sober thoughts about a dowry. Here let us mention in the first place Sztuka ["Art"], the artist's café, which was upstairs in Andriolli Passage, and where the atmospheric lighting was dimmed whenever the long-haired violinist Wasserman played Schumann's *Träumerei*. I only have a foggy memory of the Schneider, which was the famous writer's café. Before the house where it was located was demolished, I only ever dropped in there once, and not as a guest, but on a private matter to see the senior waiter, who was the father of our schoolmate, Kazio Purski. Kazio Purski died of consumption in the second or third class. In later years, as a café regular by now, I often ran into Purski's father working as a waiter in various places, but I can still see him today, weeping over his son's coffin.

The waiters I knew from the Roma made an incredible impression on me when they sat as guests at the tables of other cafés, such as the Renaissance, and ordered their colleagues who were employed there to wait on them. They wore challengingly bright jackets and colourful ties. That was their festive attire—the black work-wear dinner jackets and tail coats stayed at home, to let the weekday toil evaporate.

The Renaissance café is connected with a certain incident which to this day still fills me with pride. I have always been

GRANITO

a fan of the Renaissance era, but what I experienced at the Renaissance café on May the Third and Kościuszko Streets is more likely to qualify me for the Middle Ages. For it was here that I won a battle against the temptation of Satan. During my brief career as a teacher I was sometimes obliged—despite my innate mild nature—to slap a bad grade on a pupil, whether male or female. On this occasion the above-mentioned Satan, not in fact a very medieval character, and even less of a Renaissance one, materialized in the figure of an advocate's clerk. The devil's advocate is not always the devil himself, but this advocate's clerk undoubtedly was. He invited me to supper at the Renaissance café, known for its good food and well-stocked cellar. Not sensing a trap, I accepted the invitation. I arrived just as a large orchestra conducted by the famous Schwarzmanoff was tuning up for a potpourri from *Tosca*. Barely had I sat down with my friend the clerk at a marble tabletop, expecting at most coffee and cakes, when some Bisanzes appeared, and with suspicious obsequiousness spread out a snow-white cloth. Others brought silver tableware, and set down platters of cold meat and also fish, in both Jewish and Aryan style; meanwhile special Ober-Bisanzes opened bottles of vodka and beer—moments later they'd put down buckets with chilled champagne and the corks would start to pop...

The feast began. From a drop of vodka to a slice of ham, from a nice piece of steak to a tasty schnitzel, and the cat came out of the bag—meaning that during my conversation with the clerk it came to light that the daughter of one of the owners of the Renaissance was a pupil of mine at the gymnasium, and for her aversion to *Pan Tadeusz* she was rightly expecting a bad mark from me. So this banquet was just the artillery fire before the major assault that the satanic clerk was planning to launch at me, by offering me a bribe for a good mark. Such things were common practice in old Galicia and Lodomeria with the Grand etcetera, so in the first few years of independence people were under the illusion that they could still be applied. Not incorrectly they counted on the fact that the teaching body, just like any other body, was vapid and sinful.

I did not actually hurl an inkwell at the devil, like Martin Luther, or even a wine glass, but the reader can imagine my indignation as I threw down my snow-white napkin and called out: "The bill!" Nevertheless, Satan would not let me pay, and as I didn't want to tussle with him in the packed restaurant to the strains of a potpourri from *Madame Butterfly*, I ran out of the place without settling my account. To this day, almost a quarter of a century on, I cannot get to sleep whenever I think about it. I only manage to nod off when I remind myself that at any rate I did flunk the pupil without any qualms—or to put it in the language of Lwów, "as easy as wire".

Nowadays both she and her father, and the tempter-clerk too, are shades without a doubt. I can hear their laughter. I can hear the ghostly clatter of ivory dominoes in cafés that have been wiped from the face of the earth. The spirits of the customers summon the spirits of the commis waiters, and bid them bring newspapers in which nothing is printed except never-ending lists of the murdered citizens of Lwów. The dead are playing cards, the dead are playing billiards. The shades of the lady cashiers jingle their teaspoons against the metal trays, on which the shades of the Bisanzes serve up the sweet potion of oblivion.

Also looming up before me are eating places of a more mediocre quality: drinking dens with noisy orchestrions, beer cellars where cab drivers and cut-throats met, and where for fear of the clients who stole, the metal mugs were kept on chains, like dogs. Ham on the chain! With their colourful inn signs, with a picture of a fellow tucking into a fat goose, these taverns lure and attract the hungry and thirsty. They recommend Syrmian slivovitz, hot *krupnik*—honey liqueur, and Lwów's famous *rozolis*—rose-flavoured vodka. Old sots painted on tin, bearded King Gambrinuses[55] with their crowns at a rakish angle sit astride barrels, bursting with laughter. Frothy beer flows from the immense mugs they're holding, and also flows through the histories of conquered nations, as a sacrificial offering for the gods of annihilation. Elsewhere a mustachioed Zagłoba,[56] his belly round as a barrel, is wetting his dissipated chops with Okocim beer, and I can hear apocalyptic hiccups, and wafting from inside the bar room I can smell the fumes of fusel alcohol, Quargel cheese and gherkins, which stand in enormous jars in the window beside demijohns full of cherry brandy, marinating in dill, until they're as rancid as we shall be in this sorrowful exile... Once again I'm inhaling the noble aroma of Dalmatian wines at the Didolić and Prpić company store on Czarniecki Street—there you could happily tipple away on pearly-glitzy *zlataritsa*[57] while dreaming of sunny Dubrovnik.

I've also been pursued the world over by the aromas of Lwów's patisseries, fruit sellers, colonial stores, and Edmund Riedl and Juliusz Meinl's tea and coffee shops. Pursue is not the right word, because being pursued is unpleasant, but these aromas are delicious, though they prompt tears. Every time I returned to Lwów from "the world outside", I always found its aromas in just the same places as before. So they're probably still there today too, because smells are the hardest thing to kill or eradicate. I don't really know whether it's old age that has made me lose my nose for the fragrances of flowers and trees in exile, or whether nothing actually has a scent here? And yet Lwów's parks have followed me here with all their trees, flower beds and shrubberies. And its pharmacies, pubs and fruit shops have sailed across the ocean too—after all these years they're still here inside me, they're still alive and wonderful. Even the very memory of them is scented. Or perhaps it isn't the scent of Lwów and its magical flora at all, but the scent of our youth?

Let's drink the nectar from the glasses offered us by deceitful memory, and let's get blotto on a feast of the fragrances of Lwów. Yet the flora of the place was not just botanical. Even the sounds had a scent there. Even the surnames had an exotic odour. Listen to these: Stec, Mryc, Kipa, Tepa, Uhma, Ohly, Pazdro, Kysiak, Schubuth, Quest, Nahlik, Krzehlik, Nowosad, Najssarek Pitołaj, Sałaban, Kadernożka, Dokupil, whose daughters were called the Dokupilanki. And these: Beacock, Passakas, Garapich, Ramaszkan, Mikolasch, Chamajdes, Czaczkes, Korkis and Kikenis. Near Łyczakowski cemetery the granite tombstones were sculpted by stonemasons called Giovanni Zuliani and Son. On upper Copernicus Street, right by the electric tram depot, three locksmiths had their workshops, whose names were Oprysk ["Spatter"], Czepil ["Niggled"] and Pludra ["Breeches"]. I spent a long time wondering what sort of an ailment was niggling Mr Spatter, and in my critical years— under the influence of the muse Hypochondria—I even feared it was niggling me too. The proximity of Romania must have had an effect on the exotic diminutive forms of the local first names too, which instead of the usual Polish -ek ending, came out as: (innate modesty bids me start with my own) Józiu, Biziu, Busiu, Filu, Fulu, Milu, Dziuniu, Maniu, Luku (from Ludwik), Poldziu ([Leopold] Staff) and Weku (I don't know what that's from).

The soil of Lwów was also fertile ground for some curious originals that walked on two legs. I am not only thinking of the originals to be found in the cafés. Quaint characters, both male and female, oddballs and eccentrics added colour to our childhood like a picturesque circus, a circus free of charge, which provided as much amusement as terror. I remember, though very sketchily, "Foolish Jaś", the master of ceremonies at every decent funeral. I can remember "Hamaj-kiciu" ["Eat up, kitty"], an old fellow who used to walk along the Corso, stopping passers-by with the words: "Eat up, kitty!" Right until I left a blind, pockmarked old boy called Ignaś used to stand outside the Bernardine Church, scraping away atrociously on a fiddle. Now and then the street urchins would steal it off him, and then he would shift to another spot, where he'd have a cardboard sign hanging on his chest, on which some charitable hand had written a request for the money to buy him a new instrument. And once it had totted up, blind Ignaś would play again, and the urchins would steal his fiddle again. And so on, *da capo al fine*. After the first war a military psychopath used to buzz about on the Corso in the jacket of an Austrian Uhlan officer. He shouted, saluted and gave commands, and during Polish army parades under Mickiewicz's column he'd leap out of the crowd of sightseers in front of the marching ranks and obstruct the generals who were taking the salute. Later on "poor Lajbuś" from Chodorów arrived on the streets of Lwów to sing some very doleful Polish, Jewish and Ukrainian songs. Their main topic were Lajbuś's family squabbles and frustrated hopes. He sang about his pappy who had dollars and his mammy who had earrings, while he, poor Lajbuś, "goes without shoes".

There were also flowers of another species that grew like weeds on the rich soil of Lwów, not just the misfortunate and the addle-pated. There was for example a men's tailor called Sozański, a master at turning old clothes and removing stains. Once I took him my conscience, on which I had noticed a few little stains, but Sozański was incapable of removing them. For every national celebration this man, who had the ugliest dentition in all Lwów, changed into a *czamara*,[58] in which he looked most interesting. What's more, he wasn't the only one to wear a *czamara*. It was worn by several venerable old-style Poles in the manner of nobles, such as one of the joint owners of Musiałowicz and Janik's "breakfast room", with a nose misshapen by lupus. I no longer recall whether it was Mr Musiałowicz or Mr Janik. Right opposite their place, in the direction of Jagiellońska Street, a broad-shouldered engraver with snow-white hair spent the whole blessed week clad in a *czamara*. He sat by the window of his shop with a watchmaker's glass in his eye, engraving signet rings, and crests and monograms on the silver tableware of aristocrats who dressed like the average lawyer. But none of these *czamara*-wearers cut quite such a flamboyant figure as Sozański the tailor. One time the legal counsel Rafał Buber, who was a leading member of the Polish Socialist Party and a loyal friend of the philosopher Stanisław Brzozowski, met him on the street:

"Why are you all dressed up like that, Mr Sozański?"

"I'm off to a nosh-up to commemorate '63!"

Nosh-ups weren't the only way the anniversary of the January 1863 Uprising was celebrated in Lwów. On that day the large, but ever dwindling band of veterans of 1863 would focus the citizens' loftier sentiments on themselves. On the whole they bore up pretty well, but there was already plenty of rotten wood among them. At the head of their patriotic processions marched an unassuming, but robust civilian, Izydor Karlsbad. For it so happened that among the insurgents who had settled in Lwów, the highest rank, of captain, was held by a Jew. It was he who led the company. Behind Karlsbad a very striking ensign marched with the flag, a petty aristo in a *kontusz* and a jauntily positioned confederate's cap with a white tassel. The rest of the insurgents were mainly leaning on canes and seemed to be keeping each other's old bones and honourable scars warm. A giant stood out among them, with long shaggy locks that hadn't yet gone grey and sharp features on a clean-shaven, red-skinned face. In a coarse shirt, with a wide belt set with metal studs, this Lithuanian looked like an ancient woodland oak, like the chief of a Red Indian tribe or a highland robber as drawn by Skoczylas.[59] Many of those who took part in the Uprising no longer had families or homes, or the strength to work; some of them lived at the Doms foundation, a shelter for "writers, artists and tradesmen". Above the gate of this philanthropic ruin the noble founder had had an inscription painted in large letters that read: DES LEBENS AUSGANG ("The exit from life"). So that there would be no illusions. So that the old men, delighted by this "roof over their heads"—God forbid—would not imagine that they were going to leave this charitable abode alive, or that the light of the domestic hearth would ever shine forth for them again. The Doms foundation was the "exit" from life for the white-bearded painter Seweryn Obst, who used to stroll the Corso in a velvet beret on top of long curls that fell to his vast cloak. He looked like a figure from Henri Murger's *Bohème*,[60] and was the first person in Poland to paint Hutsul men and women on horseback.

Des Lebens Ausgang! Exitus vitae. I was not born in Lwów, but for a very long time I flirted with the idea that I'd spend the last Polish autumn of my life there, nodding quietly to myself. *Point de rêveries!* But I haven't given up the dream that for all the good I've done here on earth, for all the honey (and venom) I've penned, for the key—as the late lamented Boy-Żeleński[61] would have said—NB a broken one, which I have contributed to the keyboard of my native lingo, one day I will get my own street in Lwów. Not a major thoroughfare with mansions, banks, a court, a prison, a school, a chamber of trade and commerce, and a Turkish bath. God forbid! All I need is a small side street without any sewers and with just ten houses; one of those little alleys tucked in below the High Castle, like Sieniawa Street. And what harm would it do anyone to rename Miodowa Street as Józef Wittlin Street? Why shouldn't my contemporaries' grandchildren—young people whom I do not in the least expect to read my work—be familiar with my name, if only from the name of a side street where they will enjoy the pleasures of their day, or to put it as they do here in America, where they'll have a good time? Let it be the *rue de la Gaîté* of the Lwów of the future.

And if this modest wish can never come true, I have others up my sleeve. The whole world is full of so-called sadists. Every educated person knows that these are people who derive pleasure from tormenting their loved ones. And everyone knows that the word sadism comes from the name of a French writer, Count Donatien Alphonse François de Sade, or for short, the Marquis de Sade. He was not just a cruel man in literature but in life too, for which he was sentenced to death, pardoned and imprisoned. The revolution was raging in France, the terrors and thermidors, and the guillotine was busy chopping off the heads of other aristocrats, while our Marquis was quietly writing books entitled *Juliette, Justine, Les crimes de l'amour, La Philosophie dans le boudoir*, and other such works. Just as popular as sadism is masochism. A masochist is a sadist *à rebours*. He likes to be tormented. And he either does it himself, or has others do it, for which in a world ruled by money, a set fee is paid. In pre-Nazi Berlin I myself saw young ladies walking about the streets in high, glossy boots and red ties. In the classic land of uniforms this was the standard attire of women hired to whip masochists. Very nice, the patient reader will say, but what does all this have to do with Lwów and with your dreams? A great deal. First, because masochism comes from literature too, and secondly, because masochism can be regarded as a product of Lwów. Not that the first self-tormentors were born in the city, but because from 1848, after the so-called Spring of Nations, the tough job of police chief was performed here by a one-eyed Austrian writer called Sacher-Masoch.* He wrote novels which nobody reads nowadays. I haven't read them either, but I am told that there is an awful lot of masochism in them. In view of this fact, I have not lost the hope that my own humble name will be immortalized in a similar manner. Perhaps one day some new, innocent perversion will come into being, whose practitioners will be nothing but imitators of characters invented by me. People will say of them: "They're wittlinists!", just as they talk of sadists or masochists.

The scandalized reader may be heartened by a reminder of the fact that before Sacher-Masoch there was another Austrian living and working in Lwów, by the name of Mozart. Not in fact Wolfgang Amadeus, but his son, who was also a musician. For a number of years he conducted the Cecilian Choir there.

* Several years after *My Lwów* was published, I was informed by Stanisław Vincenz that the writer was the son of the police chief. Vincenz was given this information by the writer's daughter.

And so we find plenty of curiosities in the chronicles of our city. But the greatest rarity is something that flourished in my young days, and is now dying out in our world: and that is true friendship. I had friends who were bandits, and friends who were policemen. And several friends who were priests, including Father Rękas, known throughout Poland for his radio broadcasts for the sick. For some time I was friends with the son of the city dog-catcher, Mr Zygiel. It's no challenge for us to get on well together when we belong to the same clan, ethnicity or party, when we're linked by the same likes and dislikes. Real love, friendship and comradeship only start where they blossom against the background of sometimes glaring differences and antagonisms. I do not wish to disturb the wounds on the living body of these memories, and so I won't talk about 1918.[62] I intend to give them a thorough scratching with my pen at another, less elegiac opportunity. Yet it is hard for me to pass over in silence how, during the fratricidal fighting between Poles and Ukrainians, which cut not just the actual city into two hostile halves, my old school friend Zenon Rusin, who was at the time a Ukrainian ensign, stopped the military action outside the Jesuit Garden so that I could get home across the front line. Harmony reigned among my friends, although many of them belonged to different ethnicities that were at loggerheads, and professed different faiths and views. Members of the Endecja[63] made love with Jews, socialists with conservatives, and Rusynphiles,

Moscowphiles and the like[64] with Ukrainian nationalists. In those days there weren't any communists yet, but if there had been, they'd have been sure to make love with even the socialists. Let's play at idylls. Let's have a game where since the days of our childhood nothing bad has ever happened in Lwów or in the world as a whole, for even bad news, as seen in Harasymowicz's drawings in *Wiek Nowy*, exuded light-heartedness and humour. For a very long time I was inclined to treat all Lwów's sore points with forbearance, forgetting that my Lwów, and the entire world beyond it, is one big sore point. But let's play at idylls. Let's just play games and close our eyes.

I close my eyes and I can hear the bells of Lwów ringing; each one rings differently. I can hear the splash of the fountains on the Marketplace, and the soughing of the fragrant trees, which the spring rain has washed clean of dust. It is coming up to ten o'clock, and the place is so quiet that I can recognize the people going past by their footsteps as they hurry home for dinner. I recognize the footsteps of people who ceased to walk this earth long ago. There's no one but shades clacking their heels on the well-worn pavement slabs.

I close my eyes and I can see the crowds trailing along the Corso. They're flowing down from the City Theatre, along Legionów Street, to the Savings Bank, and then onwards to Mikolasch Passage. In a wide stream they pour onto Mariacki Square, go past the Hotel George and turn into

85

Akademicka Street, then all the way to Pilecki's pharmacy at the far end. There they turn around and slowly, steadily and quietly they undulate back to the City Theatre. The dead stroll along with the living. The dead stop the living to ask for a light for their cigarettes. The playboys make passes at the ladies in bustles, ladies who have long since been shades. It's a promenade of shades. Enemies who are now brothers in death have linked arms like old friends. They stop at the corners, where chestnuts are being roasted on smoky little stoves. Above the stoves burn oil lamps with a red cross and a Tyrolean painted on the glass. Austrian dragoon officers, with monocles in their empty eye sockets, jingle their spurs. They have just emerged from Sotschek's patisserie on Mariacki Square and are now saluting some chanteuses rustling their silk. Ukrainian Sich Riflemen from 1918 go arm in arm with Polish defenders of Lwów, with the "Eaglets".[65] The spirits of the Sokóls[66] promenade beside Jewish football players from the Hasmonea club. The crowd is growing. From side streets they are joined by firemen, servants "who stood in the gateway and were lippy",[67] and young ladies who danced the *lanciers* at balls attended by Grottger[68] himself, and prima donnas who performed in Offenbach's first operettas. All the golden youth seen by Lwów in the course of the century has swarmed out onto the Corso. A black wave of people pours into the roadway and surges up to Mickiewicz's monument. A dandy in a powdered wig and a cropped tail coat breaks out of the crowd. He stands under Mickiewicz's column, where the entire *Cäcilienchor* has already lined up on the steps. Mozart's son bows to the living and the dead. He gestures with his baton, and Mariacki Square, packed tight with the silent throng, resounds with a song from 1914: "On a rainy, gloomy day"… Just then on the roof of Dittmar & Co's store the illuminated sign comes on: "BAJKA". It lights up once, and goes out. Suddenly there's a piercing whistling noise. It's Sacher-Masoch and Captain Tauer, giving the signal to the mounted police, who are lurking in Wałowa Street. The clatter of hooves rings out against the cobblestones, and the policemen break up the crowd with their sabres. Without a sound, the hounded spectres flee in all directions, but at once they reassemble, form a herd and mass together—and the normal traffic prevails again on the Corso, a regular wave of people, a carefree promenade. The silent phantoms glide towards the City Theatre, then return from there to flow into Akademicka Street again. And so it goes on and on, to and fro, to and fro, ad infinitum, until the end of time.

Riverdale, New York, 1 May 1946

TRANSLATOR'S NOTES TO
MY LWÓW

1   *UNRRA*: United Nations Relief and Rehabilitation Administration, the post-war international aid agency.
2   *"Forefathers' Eve"*: (*Dziady* in Polish) is a pre-Christian Slavic feast to commemorate the dead, attended by the living and the souls of their ancestors.
3   *Kiliński Park*: Jan Kiliński (1760–1819), a cobbler by trade, was a commander under the leadership of Tadeusz Kościuszko (1746–1817) and led the Uprising of 1794 in Warsaw against the Russian occupation.
4   *Mayor Ciuchciński*: Stanisław Ciuchciński (1841–1912), tinsmith and public benefactor, was mayor of Lwów from 1907 to 1911.
5   *kiczki*: a game in which a player propels a stick upwards, and then hits it in mid air to make it spin and fly farther.
6   *"Hill… Teofil Wiśniowski and Józef Kapuściński"*: the leaders of a Polish independence conspiracy aiming to incite an uprising in Galicia; on 31 July 1847 they were executed by the Austrians on this site.
7   *Stanisław Ignacy Witkiewicz*: (1885–1939), known as Witkacy, was a leading Polish playwright, novelist, painter, photographer and philosopher.

8 *Racławice Panorama*: a monumental circular painting, depicting a famous battle that took place during the 1794 Uprising. It is now located in Wrocław and is a rare example of a "cyclorama", a genre of mass culture that was popular in the nineteenth century.

9 *ŁD tram*: the line ran from Łyczaków to the station (Dworzec in Polish).

10 *Baczewski*: Józef Adam Baczewski (1829–1911) was a legendary figure in Lwów, a wealthy industrialist who owned a vodka factory and fought in the January 1863 Uprising.

11 *grajzlernik*: Slavonicized form of *Greissler*, the Austrian word for grocer.

12 *Congress Kingdom*: the official name of the part of Poland incorporated into the Russian Empire.

13 *Schlussrocke*: "Body coats", an old-fashioned word found mostly in Austrian, rather than German publications.

14 *Schwarzgelberen*: (German), literally "black-and-yellows", the Austrian imperial colours, described people with pro-Habsburg political sympathies.

15 *Czerwień Towns region*: or "Red Cities" (*Grody Czerwieńskie*), the historical term for territory fought over by the Kingdom of Poland and the Grand Duchy of Ruthenia in the tenth to eleventh centuries.

16 *dezenter*: local slang for *dezerter*, meaning "deserter".

17 *River Pełtew*: Polish for what is now called by its Ukrainian name, Poltva River.

18 *"veterans' ball"… kisser*: allusion to a Lvovian song called "The Veterans' Ball", which ended with a punch-up.

19 *"Strzelnica"*: the name of this club means a shooting range.

20 *Gabriela Zapolska*: (1857–1921) was an actress, playwright and novelist whose satirical plays made fun of the petty bourgeoisie.

21 *Sous*: literal translation of the Polish *pod* meaning "under"; shops, inns and restaurants were traditionally described as being "under" [the sign of] e.g. the Emperor Titus, the Holy Spirit, the Basilisk,

etc., because of the emblems or signs over the doorway featuring their patron or symbol.

22 *"honorary"… honourable*: in Polish, *honorowy* means both "honorary" and "honourable", so Wittlin repeats it to ironical effect.

23 *Gorgonowa*: Rita Gorgonowa (b. 1901) was a governess, the central figure in one of interwar Poland's most infamous and sensational murder cases.

24 *Pacyków Lewickis*: a family famous for its faience factory.

25 *"The Oath of Jan Kazimierz"*: the Lwów Oath was sworn in 1656, in the Latin Cathedral, by King Jan Kazimierz during the "Deluge", or Swedish invasion, and entrusted the Polish-Lithuanian Commonwealth to the Blessed Virgin Mary, as a way of inciting the whole nation to resist the invaders.

26 *Juliusz Kleiner's… Imperatoris*: Kleiner (1886–1957) was a historian of Polish literature who took his doctorate in the days of the Austro-Hungarian Empire, thus "under the auspices of the Emperor".

27 *"Jawohl… sind schlecht"*: (German) "Indeed, Your Majesty! The singers are good, it's just the choruses that are bad."

28 *Mendogs or Gedymins*: Mindauas and Gediminas were medieval Grand Dukes of Lithuania.

29 *Wanda*: Princess Wanda was the daughter of Krakus, the legendary founder of Kraków, and drowned herself in the River Vistula rather than be forced to marry a German prince.

30 *Stanisław Przybyszewski*: (1868–1927) was a novelist, dramatist and poet associated with the Symbolist movement, and also a famous womanizer, with an interest in the philosophy of Nietzsche and in Satanism.

31 *Aleksander Fredro*: (1793–1876) was a poet and playwright of the Romantic era.

32 *Dziurdzio*: Polish spelling for a Romanian equivalent of the name George (in Polish, Jerzy).

33 *hospodar Miron Mohyła*: also known by his Romanian name, Miron Barnovschi-Movilă (d. 1633), was the ruler of Moldavia from 1626 to 1629. *Hospodar* is a Slavonic term for a lord or master.

34 *"Ah… gondolas"*: quotation from an aria in Johann Strauss's operetta *Eine Nacht in Venedig* (1863).

35 *Henryk Grossman… Eastern Fair*: Grossman (1881–1950) was an economist and historian. The Eastern Market (1921–39) was a huge annual trade fair, exhibiting Polish and foreign industry, and aimed at developing commercial contacts with the countries to the east of Poland.

36 *Golden Rose Synagogue… demolition*: named after Róża (Rosa) Nachmanowicz, daughter-in-law of its founder. Róża was influential and apparently mediated with the Jesuits for the restitution of the Synagogue when it was handed over to them by royal decree. After her death in 1637, she featured in various legends of martyrdom. According to one, she offered the Bishop of Lwów her entire fortune to buy back the Synagogue; the bishop agreed, but when he demanded that she become his lover, she committed suicide. It was destroyed by the Nazis in 1943.

37 *Stefan Starzyński*: (1893–1939) was the mayor of Warsaw who refused to leave the city when it was attacked by the Nazis in September 1939, but instead bravely sustained public morale during the Siege of Warsaw. He was imprisoned and shot by the Germans in December 1939.

38 *Emil Kipa*: (1886–1958) was a Polish historian and diplomat.

39 *"rendezvous sycamore"*: refers to the love poem *Laura and Filon* (1780) by Franciszek Karpiński (1741–1825).

40 *Equine Casino*: the colloquial name for the Nobleman's Casino, which was in a palatial neo-baroque mansion on Mickiewicz Street. Its members were rich landowners, including horse breeders, hence the nickname. It was a social club for gamblers, but also a political institution of right-wing, nationalist persuasion.

41 *Agenor, Count Gołuchowski… "October Diploma"*: Gołuchowski (1812–75) was a conservative politician who wrote the 1860 October Diploma, which attempted to increase the power of the conservative nobles by giving them more power over their own lands through a programme of aristocratic federalism.

42 *Jabłonowski*: Stanisław Jan Jabłonowski (1634–1702), a Polish noble-man and magnate, was Great Crown Hetman, i.e. commander-in-chief during the Swedish invasion known as the Deluge.

43 *Franciszek Smolka*: (1810–99) was a lawyer, liberal politician, public benefactor and president of the Austrian parliament.

44 *Kornel Ujejski*: (1823–97) was a Polish Romantic poet and patriot.

45 *the greatest count in Polish drama*: The statue of Fredro is now located in Wrocław.

46 *sukmana-clad hero… Bartosz Głowacki*: a *sukmana* is a traditional woollen peasant coat. Wojciech Bartosz Głowacki (1758–94) led the peasant volunteer infantry during the Kościuszko Uprising of 1794, and famously captured a Russian cannon by putting out the fuse with his hat.

47 *Maria Konopnicka*: (1842–1910) was a poet, novelist, children's writer, translator, journalist, critic and campaigner for women's rights and Polish independence.

48 *Syrokomla*: Władysław Syrokomla (1823–62) was a Polish-Lithuanian Romantic poet, writer and translator.

49 *'Who are you?' – 'A little Pole!'*: the patriotic verse "Catechism for a Polish child" by Władysław Bełza (1847–1913) is a Polish classic.

50 *Laskownicki's organ*: Bronisław Laskownicki was the editor-in-chief of *Wiek Nowy*.

51 *Marchołt*: a demon from Slavonic mythology.

52 *Tadeusz Miciński and Sar Péladan*: Miciński (1873–1918) was an expressionist, mystical poet. Joséphin (Sar) Péladan (1858–1918) was a French Rosicrucian and occultist.

53 *"Skamander"*: a group of leading experimental poets founded in 1918, whose members included Julian Tuwim, Antoni Słonimski, Jarosław Iwaszkiewicz, Jan Lechoń and Kazimierz Wierzyński. Tuwim and Lechoń both wrote the words for cabaret songs, which prompted Jan Stur to accuse them of degrading poetry.

54 *Stanisław Brzozowski*: (1878–1911), was a poet, critic and philosopher of the Young Poland modernist era (from about 1890 to 1918).

55 *Gambrinuses*: Gambrinus is a legendary king associated with the invention of beer, and often used as an icon to represent it.

56 *Zagłoba*: a popular character from Henryk Sienkiewicz's *Trilogy* (1884–8), an adventurer fighting for the Polish-Lithuanian Commonwealth, to some extent comparable with Falstaff as a literary figure.

57 *zlataritsa*: a Croatian white wine.

58 *czamara*: a traditional men's coat, similar to the *kontusz*, and regarded in the nineteenth century as patriotic Polish attire.

59 *Skoczylas*: Władysław Skoczylas (1883–1934), painter and sculptor, was regarded as founder of the Polish school of woodcut engraving.

60 *Henri Murger's Bohème*: Murger (1822–61) was a French novelist, whose *Scènes de la vie de Bohème* (1851) was the basis for Puccini's opera *La Bohème*.

61 *Boy-Żeleński*: Tadeusz Boy-Żeleński (1874–1941), doctor, critic, playwright, essayist, satirist and translator from French, was a major figure in the Young Poland literary movement, and a victim of the Nazi massacre of Lwów's professors.

62 *about 1918*: in November 1918 forces of the West Ukrainian People's Republic attacked Lwów. The conflict lasted until May 1919, when the Polish Army defeated them.

63 *Endecja*: the National Democracy political movement, which was far to the right, nationalist and generally anti-Semitic.

64 *Rusynphiles, Moscowphiles and the like*: participants in a political and cultural movement of West Ukrainian Russophiles, who in the nineteenth and early twentieth centuries held that the people of Galicia were descended from the same roots as the Russians.

65 *"Eaglets"*: the Lwów Eaglets were teenage soldiers who defended the city during the Polish-Ukrainian war of 1918–19.

66 *Sokóls*: the Sokół ("Falcon") movement was a youth sports organization that existed in several Slavonic countries and promoted pan-Slavism as well as physical and moral training.

67 *"who stood… lippy"*: the origin of this quote is obscure, possibly from a well-known joke or comedy sketch.

68 *Grottger*: Artur Grottger (1837–67), one of Poland's leading Romantic painters of the nineteenth century, studied in Lwów.

The translator wishes to thank Professor Wojciech Ligęza of the Jagiellonian University for his generous and invaluable help with many details of this text.

PHILIPPE SANDS

My Lviv

*... go breathless, go to Lwów, after all
it exists, quiet and pure as
a peach. It is everywhere.*

ADAM ZAGAJEWSKI,
To Go to Lwów
Translated by Renata Gorczyńska

I

I CAME TO LVIV MANY YEARS after Józef Wittlin. He arrived in 1906, when the city was called Lemberg, a jewel of diverse cultures in the golden crown of the Austro-Hungarian Empire. By the time he left, a decade and a half later, the empire was gone, the city was known as Lwów, and it was in Poland. When I arrived in 2010 it was no longer a home for Poles, Jews or Ukrainians (or Ruthenians, as they were once known). Now it was called Lviv, located on the western edge of the Ukraine, a country being pulled east by Russia and west by the European Union, at risk of tearing in the middle. The buildings remained, occupied by others.

Through all the changes the city hasn't moved. The cathedrals, palaces and tenements remain, a remnant of Middle Europe, lifted from the set of Orson Welles' film, *The Third Man*, caught between outstretched hills and a green and bustling metropolis that hums to the sound of trams driven by ladies in headscarves, a place where the smell of coffee lingers. I could have walked the streets in ignorance of what was gone, if I had wanted to. I could have chosen to turn away from the stories stuffed into the cracks of each building, or what was hidden behind freshly plastered walls. I could have averted my gaze, but I didn't want to. Observing with care was part of the reason for being there, seeking out what was left, traces of what came before.

My first impression, on a brilliant autumn day, was of the old airport building. The now-shuttered *Sknyliv* aerodrome opened in 1923, and when I arrived it welcomed me with its marble columns, wooden doors and little cubicles in which officials barked orders at us, even as they wore oversized green hats. I came with an invitation in hand. Would you deliver a lecture at the city's historic university? "It's older than Harvard", it was whispered. The subject? My work on international law and justice, the cases in which I was involved in courts around the world, that touched on matters of "genocide"—the destruction of groups—and "crimes against humanity"—the killing of individuals in large numbers.

I could say that I made the trip to give a lecture, but that would not be entirely truthful. I travelled for another reason, namely that my grandfather was born in the city, in 1904. Leon Buchholz called it Lemberg when he spoke in German, Lwów in Polish. Lemberg, Lwów, Lviv, Leopolis, לעמבערג (in Yiddish), the City of Lions, whatever you want to call it, I understood it to be a part of my hinterland, one that was buried deep because Leon would never speak of that past. His long silence hid the wounds of a family that was left and then lost, but from the moment I set foot in the place it felt familiar, a part of me, a place I had missed and where I felt comfortable.

"What haunts are... the gaps left within us by the secrets of others", the psychologist Nicolas Abraham wrote. Leon's secret was that he came from a huge family, one that was centred in Lemberg and its environs, literally dozens of uncles, aunts, cousins, nephews and distant relatives. The family grew and even prospered until 1939, when war returned to the city. Within six years, by the spring of 1945, he was the last member of that family to be standing, the only survivor from the city and Galicia. I knew him as a man alone, first an exile from Lwów and then, in 1939, banished from Vienna. I had a copy of his expulsion order, signed by a judge:

The Jew Buchholz Maurice Leon is required to leave the territory of the German Reich by December 25, 1938.

He was expelled because he was deemed to be stateless. He made his way to Paris, and later he was joined by his daughter and then, even later, by his wife. Over the years he became the proud Frenchman that I knew, as Lemberg faded into a not-to-be-talked-about past. He drew a sharp line across the middle of his century, an impenetrable line that I knew from early childhood was one that was not to be crossed. He never talked to me of Lemberg, and I never asked, not about the place or the family.

In this way he was the real reason I travelled to visit the city of which I knew little. Books, maps, pamphlets and photographs offered points of information, as did his personal papers, which I only came to see for the first time after I had agreed to make the trip. I made use of a fine website, hosted by the Centre for the Urban History of East Central Europe, an institution dedicated to further the understanding of the city's troubled history, its streets and buildings, its lively intellectual heft, its diverse academic and cultural roots. On this website you feel you can observe the levers of power work their changes: the first years of the twentieth century were truly blood-stained, as control of the city changed no less than eight times in just three decades between September 1914 and July 1944. I learned that after a century and a half nestled on the eastern outskirts of the Austro-Hungarian Empire, the capital of the "Kingdom of Galicia and Lodomeria and the Grand Duchy of Kraków with the Duchies of Auschwitz and Zator" passed into Russian hands, then reverted to Austria, then became the capital of the short-lived Western Ukrainian Republic (three weeks!), then part of Poland, then in short order the Soviet Union, Germany and once again the Soviet Union. Today Lviv lies in Ukraine, at a midpoint of imaginary lines that connect Riga to Athens, Prague to Kiev, Moscow to Venice. Lviv is on a fault line, one that divides east from west, north from south. In all my visits this is the fact one is not allowed to forget: it is a city on the edge of many places, a space of constant insecurity.

Before I travelled, on that first occasion, a colleague in Warsaw sent me a photocopy of a slim volume. This was Józef Wittlin's *Mój Lwów*, published in 1946 when the author was an émigré living in America. It was in Polish, a language I do not comprehend, but I was able to appreciate the grainy black-and-white photographs that showed the buildings for which I understood Wittlin to have had a special fondness. I came to learn that the best way to wander this black-and-white city—if you really want a sense of history—is to do it with four maps in your pockets: pre-war Austro-Hungarian, interwar Polish, wartime German and modern Ukrainian. In this way you can follow the changing names of the places and streets. The great Opera House, a central point of reference, has not moved an inch in the century since it was built, yet the changing names of the streets on which it is located tell their story: the *Traviata* I attended would previously have been heard on Karl Ludwig Strasse and Hetman Gasse, then on ul. (ulica—Street) Legionów and ul. Hetmańska, then on Adolf-Hitler-Ring and today on Prospekt Svobody.

The streets got under my skin. I've returned each year for the last six, sometimes more than once. I've brought my mother, son, aunt and brother, and friends (the one holdout is my wife, who says she will only come once my need to return has run its course). What was it that brought me back? The question is rather easy to answer: I returned because of the darkness, not in spite of it, pulled like a mosquito to blood. It felt like home, a place of origin, where family began. The buildings, the sounds, the trams (and their drivers), the pickles (is there anything in Lviv that cannot be pickled?), the many varieties of borscht, the gloomy side streets, the cobblestones, the old advertisements that poke their way through cracks in the plaster, the man who sells cacti (how can you not love a city in which the sale of small spiny plants still draws a crowd?), the chess tables that suddenly appear on festive days, the cold wind, the sun, the hills, the vodka and, most of all, the multitude of places where blood was spilled. Lviv is an assault on the senses and the imagination. Much has been hidden, but nothing has been lost, not completely, especially if you are willing to do your homework and search carefully.

By the time of my second visit, a year after the first, I had found a translation of Wittlin's book into Spanish, a language I barely understand but which has some similarity to French, which I do speak. So it offered a little more information I could understand, with the help of my friend Adriana, who visited with me on one occasion and offered a translation service and companionship on streets and trains. Published by Wittlin's daughter, I liked the lime-green cover, which made the book's contents—and somehow the city too—even more attractive. With Wittlin's Spanish words I began to glean the sense of idyll, the nooks and crannies in which he found refuge and sustenance. His words came to life, and the fact that they described the streets on which my grandfather walked—at the time on which he walked them—added to the magic. Wittlin's idyll refracted that of my grandfather's. With Wittlin's help I could imagine myself in the city with Leon, long after he left, holding his hand. So lyrical, so full of life and of energy and hope, Wittlin encouraged the imagination to be fertile and generous.

Thus did Józef Wittlin's *Lwów* merge into mine, two indistinguishable places, his then, mine now. Gradually my powers of resistance diminished. Wittlin filled out the spaces, the city his friend Joseph Roth described as a place of "blurred borders". Even if my mind's image of the city is in black and white, I could see it truly as a firmament of bright colours in fiery competition, feeling the parry and the thrust of the "red-white", the "blue-yellow" and the "black-gold", the tensions between the Polish, Ukrainian and Austrian.

Successive occupations worked their mischiefs. The Jewish population was erased by act of extermination, and much of the Polish population that remained after that terrible period chose to depart during the Soviet occupation. The character of modern Lviv, now with its strong Ukrainian accent, would surely seem different to Wittlin. The city I came to know was blue and yellow. Yet, occasionally, in the people too, the hint of what came before was allowed to be ignited. It happened after that first lecture, and then again with subsequent talks I have given: a student would approach, linger, open a conversation, offer a hint about family origins. "Your lecture was significant for me personally", I would be told quietly. I understood what was being said: ancestral origins, especially if they were of a Polish or Jewish hue, were not matters to be proclaimed from the rooftops.

II

The streets I came to know would be familiar to Józef Wittlin. In the old centre they formed the same patterns and shapes, and the shadows created by the buildings fell much as they did a century ago. The nasty, cheap Soviet-era blocks that came to the city three decades after Wittlin left were on the periphery. And even if the identity and dress of those who walked the streets was different, the monsters that Wittlin and Leon would rather forget were present and discernible.

So was the coffee, the excellence of which was truly one of the city's enticements. I am partial to coffee, and that surely helped foster my positive feeling about the place. As in Wittlin's time, each of the many cafés seemed to have its own clientele and style. The *Europejska*, the *Sztuka* and the *Renaissance* were gone, along with the waiters drawn from the community of German settlers, yet the taste of

Vienna remained. A good place to start each morning—they opened early—was *Svit Kavy* on Katedralna Square (plac Kapitulny), close to the George Hotel where I liked to stay (always on the first floor, not yet fully renovated, in a room behind a thick wooden door, the kind that was opened with a large, old-fashioned key).

Svit Kavy is tucked into a small square between the "black layer cake" and stone lions of the Boim family chapel and the eighteenth-century Latin Cathedral. This was one of the city's three cathedrals, now adorned with a brass plaque to commemorate the first ever visit of a Polish pope, to a city that was no longer Polish, in a formal sense (even if John Paul II's liturgy was attended by over a million people). Here in *Svit Kavy* the coffee was rich and creamy, served with a single, small glass of water. If the season was right there was plum strudel (but only on some days of the week) served with a generous serving of warm crème anglaise. There was no better place to start the day, anywhere in the world. Climb the stairs to the first floor, smell the roast, sit near a window, watch the locals, listen in on the visitors, do your emails, work out your maps, plan the morning route. In this place it wasn't difficult to connect to the smell of wild cherry (*czerecha*) from Wittlin's day—a fruit long disappeared, like the old waiters. In this place you could be embraced by the cup of gall that was the city of Lwów.

One of the things I liked about Wittlin was that he seemed not to have lost the capacity to hope. In his long exile he dreamt that one day a street might be named in his honour. He didn't expect a major thoroughfare, had no desire for a palace, a prison or a school, or even a Turkish bath. He had no experience of the concentration camp at Janowska, within the city limits, or the Citadel, closer to the city centre, where tens of thousands were murdered (it's now a five-star hotel, which says something about the city's engagement with history, a bit like turning a wing of the Auschwitz Camp into a Club Med). No, Wittlin's dream was to be remembered by something more modest, "a small side street without any sewers and with just ten houses". He hoped for one of those narrow alleys situated under the Union Hill, mentioning Miodowa Street (Medova Street), a word that means "honey". I knew the street, located in the triangle between the Opera House and Union Hill. Branching off ul. Zamarstynowska (Zamarstynivs'ka Street), this was not a place of sweetness, but it was a good place to start a walking tour, in the city of many dark attractions.

The first time I passed Honey Street I was in search of a building. It had been the home, many decades ago, in Wittlin's time, of an impoverished Polish student called Rafael Lemkin. In 1923 Lemkin lived on ul. Zamarstynowska, a student at the law faculty at the university of Lwów, the institution at which many years later I would deliver lectures. Located on the wrong side of the tracks, the building was dark and gloomy, in need of care and attention. Back then, when it may have been brighter, Lemkin was not known in the city, but in 1945 he was named in an op-ed in the *New York Times* and in an article in *Le Monde*, famous as the man who invented the word "genocide" (achieved by amalgamating the Greek word *genos* (tribe, or race) with the Latin word *cide* (killing)). The term emerged as a consequence of Lemkin's meticulous examination of Nazi decrees, which he gathered from across Europe between 1941 and 1943 whilst he was in exile, first in Sweden and later in the United States. Lemkin parsed thousands of documents in the search for an answer to a question that troubled him: was there an underlying plan to explain the pattern of Nazi behaviour across occupied Europe, including Poland and Lwów? He concluded that there was, and the pattern concerned acts that were directed against people not in their individual capacity but as members of groups. "New conceptions require new terms", he explained in his book *Axis Rule in Occupied Europe*, published in America in 1944.

In accepting an invitation to deliver a lecture on the origins of "genocide", I had not known that the man who invented the word had once lived in Lwów. He spent five years in the city, from 1921 to 1926, and it was in this period, in a classroom at the law faculty, that an exchange with an unnamed professor catalysed his legal creativity. In this way, as well as in others, the word "genocide" has an intimate connection with my Lviv, even if it is not one that is celebrated. I have written about this in my book *East West Street*.

I sought out Lemkin's student records, and located them in the State Archive of Lviv Oblast, near Muzeina Square. Just north of the Town Hall, the square is home to an enticing flea market, one that hawks badges, records, postcards, newspapers and books from across the ages, the detritus of the city's terrible twentieth century. If you were lucky, as my son was, you might find a Soviet-era cuckoo clock; if you were very lucky you could get some high-end Nazi memorabilia, although actually buying it wasn't easy. On one occasion I spotted the familiar shape of a dark-green *Stahlhelm*, a steel helmet with a swastika on one side and an SS symbol on the other. As I approached, in a state of vague surprise, never having seen such a thing outside of a film, the item was removed and placed out of sight. The owner shooed me away, loudly.

The entrance to the State Archive of Lviv Oblast is on this square. The Archive occupies a part of the dilapidated, mouldy eighteenth-century building that abuts the former Dominican monastery, a wing of the Baroque Church of the Blessed Eucharist. Now a Ukrainian-Greek Catholic church, it served, during Soviet times, as a museum of religion and atheism. I would not have found this place but for the diligent assistance of two very able doctoral students from the law faculty. Ivan Horodyskyy (who has since helped establish a centre for human rights in the city) and Ihor Leman, both eager to learn more about Lemkin and other lost colleagues from their law faculty, helped me

disinter student records from their place of burial in the Archive's crypt. Dozens of leather-bound volumes appeared on the tables of the reading room, one atop the other, observed from a distance by a curious nun in a grey habit. Each volume contained hundreds of forms, alphabetically arranged, each page filled in by hand by a student, identified as Polish, or Mosaic (Jewish), or, less frequently, Ruthenian (Ukrainian).

On one of these pages, untouched for nine decades after he signed it, we deciphered the address written out by Lemkin: 21 ul. Zamarstynowska. Here he was living in October 1923. Two decades later the building was in the city's Jewish ghetto, just beyond the gates under the railway bridge that served as the ghetto entrance. Through these gates passed a long line of citizens on their way to mass extermination at Bełżec, by gas. The lawyers, doctors, writers, poets, professors and waiters who travelled there came from Wittlin's daily life, many named in his essay. Tens of thousands of personal genocides, each passing the house of the man who invented the word, although they wouldn't have known that fact.

Such forlorn streets inevitably unleashed the darkest of thoughts, and so did the buildings. Between the railway bridge and Miodowa Street was a large school, now used on Sundays as a market for old postcards and banknotes. The first time I stood in the courtyard behind the school, in the autumn of 2012, I had no idea what that yard had

been used for. Now armed with that knowledge, that this vast and empty place was a gathering point for thousands of final journeys, it was difficult not to put oneself into the minds of those there gathered, fearful about what might be coming. It was also difficult to avoid a feeling of anger, for there was not the slightest indication of what the function of this space had once been, no list of names of those who passed through it. It was a place of terrible silences, the expression of a conscious desire not to remember.

III

In September 1914 "the Russians captured Lwów" and the city was overtaken by panic. Wittlin passes gently over that moment, telling us only that "the shooting-club mayor Neumann fled to Vienna". Neumann was not alone in making that westward journey. Amongst the tens of thousands who left the city as Lvovians but arrived in Vienna as *Ostjuden* (Eastern Jews, a pejorative term) was a ten-year-old boy with large ears, accompanied by his sister and portly, well-coiffed mother. This was my grandfather Leon with his mother Malke, heading to Vienna from their home at 12 Szeptyckich Street. The address was on an English translation of Leon's birth certificate, prepared in 1938 by Bolesław Czuruk, esteemed professor of Slavonic literature at the University of Lwów. Later he helped hundreds of Lwów Jews to obtain false papers during the German

occupation, an act that did not prevent the Soviets from incarcerating him after the war.

Today Szeptyckich Street is known as Sheptyts'kykh Street. It lies close to St George's Cathedral, the Greek Catholic Metropolitan Church that stands atop one of the hills that overlooks the city. A colossal structure, it hovers ethereal as a guardian angel. Each night the edifice is lit up, turned into a bright star.

The search for the place of my grandfather's birth—and the home he left in 1914—was not without its challenges. From the grassy square in front of St George's it was only a short walk to Sheptyts'kykh Street, more an avenue than a street, much grander than I had envisaged. (Wittlin believes that memory "falsifies everything", but surely the imagination of the unknown is an even greater falsifier?) Number 12 lay beyond a few nondescript Soviet-era buildings, a well-built brick house set back from the street. It had yellow walls, and in the late autumn a few trees stood bereft before it, without leaves. Yet the carved wooden entrance was impressive and open, and inside fine old tiles still covered the floor, the walls enjoyed a new coat of paint, dark green and white. Once a single family home, the building was now divided into flats, each front door lost behind a large metal shutter. Curious to see what an apartment looked like, I rang a bell on the ground floor. There was no answer, so I rang another. Silence. I climbed the stairs to the first floor, heard voices behind the shuttered front door, knocked gently, then more

loudly. The door half-opened and a man in his late forties peered out, wearing nothing but tight-fitting white underpants. He said he was busy, I should come back the next day.

I didn't return. Not because I was scared off by the white underpants, but because overnight I learned that I had found the wrong building on the wrong street. The city has two streets with similar names: one is a major thoroughfare that honours Andrey Sheptytsky (the Metropolitan Archbishop of the Ukrainian-Greek Catholic Church who, in November 1942, published a pastoral letter titled "Thou Shalt Not Murder", and would harbour in safety a number of Jews); the other street branches off the first, smaller and quieter, a memorial to the Metropolitan's family. Leon lived on the lesser street. Number 12 is a two-storey, late-nineteenth-century building, with five large windows on the first floor. Cadastral records revealed that it was constructed in 1878, that in June 1901 the Lemberg magistracy authorized the installation of plumbing (four toilets shared between the six apartments), and that an inn was located on the site before World War I (most likely run by my great-grandfather Pinkas, who trained in the art of distilling liquids into liquors: he died in December 1914 of a broken heart, after his son Emil went missing in action during the Russian offensive on Lemberg a few weeks earlier, a battle described at the time by the *New York Times* as "a thousandfold cosmic destruction and wrecking of human life, the most appalling holocaust history had ever known").

An elderly couple now lived in Leon's place of birth, Mr and Mrs Yevgen Tymchyshyn. Yevgen told me that he had lived in the building since childhood, that his parents moved in at some point in 1943. The Germans were in charge, the Jews were gone, he said. His wife showed me around the apartment, the tiny kitchen and the small room in which the elderly couple slept and which doubled up as a dining room. Against a background of walls lined with colourful landscapes, we drank cups of strong black tea. Yevgen rummaged around and dug up a pamphlet with a picture of his son Mykhailo, a candidate for office in Lviv with the Strong Ukraine Party. Later Ivan, my assistant whose PhD was on the Russian naval base at Sebastopol, told me that the party was on the left and pro-Russian, but that it didn't exist any more.

Political upheavals in modern Ukraine were as constant now as in the first years of the last century, but I hadn't appreciated the long shadow that Russia cast over the country and city. My visit with the Tymchyshyns coincided with yet another struggle between competing factions in Ukraine, as the eastern part of the country pulled towards Russia and the western part, led by nationalists in Lviv, pulled in favour of closer cooperation with Western Europe (a year later, in November 2013, under pressure from Russia, President Viktor Yanukovych refused to sign an association agreement with the European Union: a wave of protests erupted, followed by the *Euromaidan* revolution, the ouster of President Yanukovych who fled to Russia, the signing of the EU association agreement, Russia's takeover of Crimea and a proxy armed conflict between the two countries in the eastern part of the country).

In conversation Yevgen and I avoided such matters. Instead we went and stood on the small balcony at the back of the apartment. He donned an old military cap, from the Soviet era, and behind us St George's Cathedral loomed large. It glowed in the autumn sun, like a giant peach, probably as it did in the years of Wittlin, as Leon beheld it. It was truly a powerful impression, "like a symbol of heavenly triumph over the torments of earthly existence".

One of the worst places for earthly torments would have been the Brygidki Prison, which lay in the long shadow of St George's, close to Horodoska Street. The building started as a nunnery in the seventeenth century. From September 1939 it was used as a place of detention by the Soviet NKVD, a fact one was not allowed to forget in modern Lviv. Two years later, from the summer of 1941, it was run by the Gestapo, a fact that generates less attention. Thousands were brought to this place but never left. Amongst them was a man Wittlin described as the most "highly Lvovian" of individuals, Kazimierz Bartel, a graduate of the Lwów Polytechnic, mathematician and former Prime Minister of Poland. His learning and former office offered no respite: he was taken from a cell and shot dead, supposedly on the personal order of Heinrich Himmler.

Himmler visited the city in August 1942, to spend an evening in the company of the Nazi Governor of Distrikt Galicia, Otto von Wächter, an Austrian lawyer. I think they dined together at Wächter's home, at 127 Leuthenstrasse (now Ivana Franka Street), a house I would later visit with Wächter's son Horst. It was now a centre for troubled children, with a small zoo. "A lot had to be done in Lemberg", the Governor wrote to his wife Charlotte on 16th August 1942, as he travelled back from Kraków to meet with Himmler. Their meeting was the subject of a written memorandum sent a few days later by Himmler to Dr Stuckart, the *Reich* Minister of the Interior in Berlin. "I recently was in Lemberg," Himmler explained, "and had a very plain talk with the governor, SS-Brigadeführer Dr Wächter. I openly asked him whether he wants to go to Vienna… Wächter does not want to go to Vienna."

Lemberg had its attractions even in the midst of war and occupation, as final solutions were prepared and then implemented.

IV

"Where are you now, park benches of Lwów", Wittlin asks wistfully from the safety of New York. Are you "blackened with age and rain, coarse and cracked like the bark of medieval olive trees?"

The benches are exactly where they were on the day Wittlin left the city, nearly a century ago. There was one bench I often sat on, with its matching rubbish bin, both in Art Nouveau style, here in the Ivan Franko Park, under the gaze of St George's Cathedral. Today the park's slopes are named in honour of Ukraine's leading poet, a writer of realist prose and murder mysteries, a man who died impecunious in the city, exactly one hundred years ago. Franko's stock had risen in the intervening years, and he was now celebrated with a large statue that towered over the park and allowed him to gaze directly into the upper windows of the building that was once the *Landtagsgebäude* (Parliament) of the Austro-Hungarian Empire. Now it is his building, so to speak, the Ivan Franko University, formerly the Jan Kazimierz University of Lwów.

In Wittlin's day the park was known as *Tadeusz Kościuszko* Park, in honour of a Polish national hero who fought in the American War of Independence. The poet tells us the name would never have crossed the lips of a true Lvovian, with his "innate abhorrence of solemnity". For such people it was known more simply as the Jesuit Garden, a place of frilly skirts and Royal-Imperial military music, and of blackened benches. The music and the skirts were gone, but the benches remained, resolute and strong.

If you were sitting on one of them on the 1st of August in 1942, you might have caught a glimpse of a long motor-cade, a line of black Mercedes bringing to the building's entrance the Nazi Governor of the Gouvernement-General, Hans Frank. He arrived to deliver a speech in the debating chamber of the former *Landtagsgebäude*, which by then was— as it still is today—the university Aula, the main hall. In this impressive place he announced to those politely gathered that new measures were being taken against the Jews and the Poles of the city and the surrounding areas. Within days Frank's effort, with the support of Wächter, had swept tens of thousands of the city's residents to their deaths.

One amongst them was the lordly and aristocratic "figure" of Ostap Ortwin, editor and last president of the Lwów Writers Union, a man whose roar once shook the windowpanes of the *Roma* café. Does Ortwin still occupy the same vault of heaven, imagined by Wittlin? Does he read, shout, thunder and laugh at us all as we struggle to make sense of the half-empty streets of Lviv today, of the city that beats to the West-facing heart of Ukraine and still fears the return of the Russians, evicted in 1915, then as Soviets in 1941, and then again in 1991?

Long ago Ortwin would have wandered along the corridors of the *Landtagsgebäude*, now filled with the chatter and energy of young students, passing the small room that serves as the office of Professor Roman Shust, Dean of the history faculty at Lviv University. I spent a few hours here with the historian, reputed to know "everything" about the institution, a generously proportioned man with plenty of grey hair and a broad smile. He was interested in the student records I'd uncovered in the City Archives, the men (and the few women) who defined the city's connection to the rule of law a century earlier. The Germans went through all these files, he told me, one by one, page by page, looking for Jews. It was all so easy. He put his finger on the line at the top of the form, where the students entered their nationality and religion. Polish. Ukrainian. Mosaic. "Polish Jew", Lemkin wrote on his form, or maybe it was "Jewish Pole".

Lemkin's words prompted a tale about one of his teachers, Professor Maurycy Allerhand. Did I know that Allerhand lost his life just a short distance from the university to which he devoted his life? Dean Shust asked. Did I know that his cause of death in the Janowska Camp was impertinence, the crime of asking a question of a German officer as he extinguished the life of another inmate? "Have you no soul?" Allerhand asked. Four words, paid for with his life.

Dean Shust sighed as he went through the old student papers. "Poor grades," he said from time to time. This was probably because of religion, he added, a consequence of the "negative attitude" in the minds of some of the professors. Back then the teachers could decide that they wouldn't have Jewish or Ukrainian students in their classroom, or they could make them sit in the back row and stay silent. That was life in Lwów, during Wittlin's idyllic years.

The windows of Roman Shust's office overlook May the Third Street (ul. Sichovykh Striltsiv), buzzing with students. Wittlin had a special feeling for one of the cafés on this street, the *Renaissance*, where the owner offered him a culinary bribe to raise his daughter's grade. She was averse to the poetry of Adam Mickiewicz, and "Such things were common practice in old Galicia and Lodomeria." They seemed to be common still today. After one of my lectures, fortified by shots of Baczewski vodka, students of the university shared jaw-dropping stories of personal corruption, how a few hryvnias to a poorly paid university teacher—at the law faculty!—would enhance a grade. Ukrainian hryvnias were good, they explained, but euros or dollars were even better.

May the Third Street is long, but not as long or as busy as Sykstuska Street (Petra Doroshenka), which runs parallel. I came to have a special affection for this street, for it was in its elegant eighteenth- and nineteenth-century buildings that various members of the Lauterpacht family lived. This was before they were hived off into the ghetto and then, after the Great Action of August 1942, into the schoolyard that led to the rail tracks and extermination.

Hersch Lauterpacht was born in nearby Żółkiew in 1897 and moved to Lwów in 1911 with his family, to get a better education. Three decades later he was appointed to a chair in international law at the University of Cambridge. There, in the well-tended garden of his home on Cranmer Road in the summer of 1945, the eminent Lvovian, author of the first law book about an international bill of the rights of man, offered a suggestion that could change the world. To his guest—Robert Jackson, recently appointed by President Truman as chief prosecutor at the upcoming Nuremberg trial—he asked: Why not add to the list of crimes for which the defendants would be prosecuted a new one that would be called "crimes against humanity"? The words referred to the slaughter and mistreatment of individuals on a large scale. Jackson liked the idea, and within a month the new crime was introduced into the Nuremberg Statute and became a part of international law.

It struck me as remarkable that the city produced not only the man who invented the word "genocide", but also the one who catalysed the use of the term "crimes against humanity". Equally remarkable was that no one in Lviv or even the law faculty seemed to be aware of this coincidence. Professor Boris Tyshchyk, who arrived in 1953 and is the oldest surviving member of the law faculty, referred to the crushing effect of Soviet rule. "You cannot imagine what it was like to be under that," he told me, "and that is why we know nothing about all these people you are interested in." On another occasion, in the course of a seminar, I enquired of a packed room of students whether they felt themselves to be closer to Lauterpacht or Lemkin: Do you feel yourselves to be autonomous individuals or members of a group? Only one hand went up. "Ukraine is a nation, I am part of that, and that defines me," the student said. My enquiry as to whether anyone had a different view was met with silence.

Lauterpacht studied at the same law faculty as Lemkin, but a few years earlier, from 1915 to 1919. Wittlin refers only in passing to the events in that period, to November 1918. "I do not wish to disturb the wounds on the living body of these memories", he writes, a reference to fratricidal fighting between Poles and Ukrainians which cut the city and many friendships "into two hostile halves". Control of the city passed from the Austro-Hungarian Empire to a new Polish state, and in the bloody conflict that followed Lauterpacht joined patrols and manned a street barricade, to protect his family and their home. The only photograph of a barricade that I found was of Sykstuska Street. I liked the image, it reinforced my idealized sense that the origins of human rights, with Lauterpacht and Lemkin as midwives, may be traced not only to this city but to this very street.

"Let's play at idylls." Yes, let's play at idylls, let us do as Wittlin suggests and treat all of Lwów's sore points with forbearance, even if Lviv and the world beyond it is today but "one big sore point". We too can play at games, as the world erupts once more. We too can close our eyes, and imagine that beyond the dark clouds that settled over this unhappy city, a ray of light broke through, and that it still offers hope today.

v

I was curious to discover where Lauterpacht and Lemkin studied. I learned that during their time at the university the

lectures offered by the law faculty were delivered in a building that adjoined St Nicholas' Roman Catholic Church, today the Ukrainian Orthodox Church of the Protection of the Mother of God. Large and square, the building is on Hrushevskoho Street, which used to be south-west Mikołaja Street. It projected a solid nineteenth-century Austro-Hungarian presence, three storeys of authority that looked down on the daily human life. On its creamy walls I read a number of plates of different sizes, a record of the illustrious individuals who once passed through its doors. No lawyer got a mention, not Lauterpacht or Lemkin, not yet regarded as eminent Lvovians. The interior was as it was in their day, with its cramped porter's lodge and corridors lit by glass globes that hung from the ceiling. There was barely enough light to appreciate the cracked and peeling paint.

The building was now home to the Department of Biology. The centrepiece for any visitor—not marked in any guidebooks I came across—was a zoological museum that offered an unusual journey back in time, to the late nineteenth century when the artefacts began to be gathered. The collection was remarkable by any standard, transporting the visitor back to the Austro-Hungarian period, five rooms packed with butterflies and moths, vicious-toothed frogfish and other denizens of the sea, lizards and reptiles, eggs of a thousand hues and shapes, skeletons both mighty and fragile. A stuffed pelican gazed through the window and over the city, monkeys effortlessly clambered the walls,

birds perched in glass coffins. A white owl observed an eagle that struggled to imagine a way through a sheet of glass in a cabinet occupied by a bird of paradise (*Schlegelia wilsonii*), still thinking about the possibility of a journey home to Papua New Guinea. Birds such as this inspired the designers of hats, the museum curator explained. He pointed to a small black-and-yellow-feathered creature with two spiral feathers on its head. One twirled left, the other right.

In this building one could easily imagine the city as it was, a place as "Diversified, variegated [and] dazzling as an Oriental carpet." This curious biological collection attested to the variety of biological life, but it also threw up questions: where were the spaces devoted to the former residents of the city, the Greeks, Armenians, Italians, Saracens and Germans? They too were once Lvovians, celebrated by monuments and spires that reflected their cultures and lives. What of the legacy of the Polish and Jewish inhabitants whose presence had been eclipsed? What happened to those ladies who wore paradise hats? The only human face, who greeted us at the entrance—placed there by a curator with a fine sense of humour—was a porcelain doll, her lips still pink and blue eyes half open. She must have emerged from a forgotten resting place in some attic, encrusted in the remains of a beehive, a memento to Wittlin's idyllic world. The city's human past was everywhere and it was nowhere.

Yet not all had been erased. On another floor of this same building I visited the classroom in which Ivan Franko once studied, preserved more or less as it was in the late nineteenth century. In this room, or perhaps another like it along the corridor, or one floor up, also elegant and simple, bright and airy, Lauterpacht and Lemkin would have learned about the mysteries of crime and law. They sat on wooden benches, in a classroom that looked out over an internal courtyard, a place of learning and order in a city of tumult and palaces, where hierarchies were constantly being knocked over and the rules changed.

In a room like this their teacher of criminal law, the bearded Juliusz Makarewicz, delivered his last lecture on the criminal law of an Austro-Hungarian Empire in late 1918, as the empire was extinguished. Nothing if not flexible, Professor Makarewicz embraced the criminal laws of others. For the next two decades he taught the criminal law of Poland, indeed he became the father of its code of criminal procedure. As control of the city passed from one group to another, Makarewicz was open to changes, of country and of government. The students changed too, as did the laws, yet on he went into the Soviet era, into the decrees promulgated by Hans Frank, and then back once more into the laws of the Soviet age. Each time he must have adjusted his lectures, to accommodate the new reality.

Everyone paid a price in this city, including Juliusz Makarewicz, guardian of criminal procedure, arrested by the NKVD in Lvov in 1945 and banished to the eastern edges of the Soviet empire. A group of Polish professors agitated for his release and got him out. He might have been expected to leave the city and move to Poland, but no, once more the City of Lions exerted its magical pull and he was unable to resist. He returned to the house he'd built near the old law faculty building, on upper Drahomanova Street, now a place of psychiatric convalescence for traumatized children. He lived his last years under Soviet domination, offered occasional lectures at the law faculty and took a final journey to the Łyczakowski cemetery.

This I learned from the venerable Professor Petro Rabinovich, who arrived in Lviv in 1954 and has taught at the law faculty ever since. He remembered Makarewicz— they overlapped for a year—and later ploughed a solitary field as the law school's principal teacher of human rights. Introduced to me as one of only two members of the law faculty who were members of the Ukrainian Academy of Legal Sciences, a throwback to Soviet days, he offered to accompany me on a visit to the cemetery, but in the end I visited on my own. Makarewicz lies close to the poets who inspired Wittlin.

May the soil of Lwów lie gently on the professors, and on the lawyers too.

VI

I am partial to railway stations, and the main one in Lviv, built in 1904, was no exception. "The pride of every Lvovian" was a notable point of departure and arrival and it continued to impress, although not quite as richly and brilliantly as it must have a century ago. The vast "semicircular, harmoniously vaulted glass halls" retained the power of amazement, especially when an old steam train drew in. There was no longer a first-class waiting room, and someone had removed the life-size portrait of Archduke Karl Ludwig that once hung in the second-class waiting room, the one that showed him with his fair beard and Uhlan uniform. No longer were you able to watch hussar officers, or Moldovan boyars with "dark, cunning faces" and "heavy gold rings", or the dark-eyed women in "heavy silk clothing and dirty slips".[*]

Occasionally, a long-bearded Ruthenian priest might brush past, but he did not walk with faded coquettes making their way to Bucharest or Iasi to seek their luck, or alongside any "civilized travellers" making their way to the west. What I saw, in large numbers, were pockets of middle-aged men in trademark Soviet-era long leather coats, and short elderly ladies who carried bags overfilled with groceries, trundling along, in tightly drawn, flowery headscarves. For twenty-five cents travellers could get themselves a fortifying shot of vodka, served by a red-headed lady who wore a crown of white paper.

[*] Karl Emil Franzos, *Aus Halb-Asien: Land und Leute des östlichen Europas*, vol. 2 (Berlin, 1901), in Alois Woldan, "The Imagery of Lviv in Ukrainian, Polish, and Austrian Literature", John Czaplicka, *Lviv: A City in the Crosscurrents of Culture* (Cambridge: Harvard University Press, 2005), p. 85.

It was from this place that Leon left Lwów for Vienna, in 1914. Lauterpacht followed five years later. In 1922 Wittlin took the train to Kraków, and Lemkin followed him to Warsaw in 1926. Leon returned in 1923, to obtain the Polish passport to which he was entitled as a result of the agreement reached at Versailles in the summer of 1919. He spent a few weeks in the city, to which his mother had returned, and left for the last time on 24th August 1923, on a train to Kraków, like Wittlin. The station was a museum of the Lvovian diaspora, a place from which idyll and memory were scattered across the world, settling here and there, in faraway places.

It was also a point of arrival. Hans Frank arrived here in July 1942, in the private carriage of a private train, on a fine summer's day, greeted by the ringing of church bells and a military orchestra, and a multitude of children waving little flags in red, white and black. He arrived with a speech, one that unleashed murder on the families and friends of those who stayed behind, because they couldn't leave or didn't wish to. Leon, Lauterpacht and Lemkin were touched by Frank's generosity.

The journeys I took from the station were more local, to the nearby town of Zhovkva, formerly known as Żółkiew. This was the small town where Leon's mother— my great-grandmother—was born in 1870, and where Hersch Lauterpacht was born a quarter of a century later. Coincidentally, they lived on the same street, known in their day as Lembergstrasse, a long east-west street, albeit at opposite ends. Zhovkva is only about twenty-five kilometres from Lviv, but it took well over an hour to get there by slow train, as it ambled across an agricultural plain, along a wide valley hung between low, distant hills. Arriving at the small station, it was a short walk to the Jan Sobieski Castle that marked the town centre, with its Ringplatz, the nearby Dominican convent, St Lawrence's Cathedral (where Stanisław Żółkiewski and a few lesser Sobieskis were buried) and the Basilian convent. Here too was the City Hall, with its tall tower topped by a wraparound balcony from which, in the 1930s, at midday precisely each day, a policeman would emerge with a trumpet and play Chopin. Close by, behind a corrugated iron fence and much litter, stood the dilapidated, splendid seventeenth-century synagogue. On a cold autumn morning the square and the town felt faded and sad. Once a micro-civilization, a place where scholarly religious books were published, it was now a place of potholes and roaming chickens.

Two rooms in one of the castle's wings served as the town museum. To one wall were affixed a small number of dismal black-and-white photographs, small and indistinct, grainy and unfocused. They showed the effects of German occupation in the summer of 1941: armoured vehicles, grinning soldiers, a synagogue on fire. I had seen nothing like this in Lviv, and no photograph such as the one here displayed, of a Żółkiew city gate from which banners were draped.

HEIL HITLER!
Long live the Independent United Ukrainian State!

What courage to display such images! I sought out the curator, Lyudmyla Baybula, a municipal employee, who asked that I call her Luda. A forceful individual with jet-black hair and striking blue eyes, Luda had devoted herself to learning about the town's wartime years, a period during which virtually the entire Jewish population was exterminated, 3,500 people murdered on a single day. Luda told me that her interest was ignited in childhood, the consequence of time spent in the company of her grandmother, one of whose friends was an elderly Jewish lady, the last one in town.

Over a meal at a local restaurant—the menu included such delights as "scars stewed with cream sauce" and "brain fried with onion"—Luda wondered if I knew about the local mass grave. "Would you like to visit?" I would. This was the place to which 3,500 inhabitants were marched on a spring day in 1943, along an east-west street, the high street once known as Lembergerstrasse. We went in the direction of Lviv, a first kilometre and then a second, across fields, through a gate, onto a path of fine, crushed sand, into a wood of birch and oak trees with the sound of cicadas and frogs, with the smell of the earth. This was an area where Leon and Lauterpacht would once have played, the *borek*, or woods. We left the sandy path, went onto the grass and into the bushes, and then we reached a clearing in the wood.

"We have arrived," Lyudmyla said. There were ponds, two great sandpits filled with an expanse of dark water and mud and reeds that bent in the wind, a site marked by a single white stone, erected not by the town in expression of grief or regret, but as a private act of remembrance by an unnamed descendant. We sat on the grass, watched the remains of the sun fall onto the dark, still water that stretched tight across the openings of the earth. Deep down, untouched for half a century and more, lay the remains of the 3,500 people. Amongst them were members of Lauterpacht's family, and of mine. The sun warmed the water, the trees pointed upward and away from the reeds, towards an indigo sky.

Here we were, once more summoning up the ghosts of Lwów's past. "O God! God of the Poles, the Ukrainians, the Armenians, God of the Lwów Jews, totally and utterly annihilated!"

VII

If you like pickles and borscht, or are partial to meat in exceptionally large quantities, or hanker for the possibility of a dessert that surprises—think pasta shells filled generously with marinated cherries and topped with whipped cream—then you will appreciate the food in Lviv. The place to which I frequently returned was below hallowed ground and not so easy to find, the basement of the Museum of

Ideas gallery, hewn out of the bowels of the Bernardine Church, below its wild, baroque, fabulous interior. Under the massive façade of this great monument, crowned by stone monks who watched peaceably over the city, you would find a glorious dish of slow-cooked lamb with apricots and prunes, not easily forgotten.

I was introduced to the wooden tables of *Trapezna* ("refectory" in Ukrainian) on Valova Street, few in number but always busy, by Sofia Dyak, Director of the Centre for Urban History of East Central Europe. Over the years Sofia has served as guide and interpreter, as historian, as adviser on issues large and small, of matters culinary, geographic and political. Was there a building or street whose history she didn't know? Was there anyone in the city she didn't have access to? My affection for Lviv was in large part a product of her big heart and intellect, coupled with a generosity and a willingness to share gentle and sardonic insights. Sofia knew what lay below the surface, and happily shared the information with a twinkle of mischief. She was the great contextualizer, fully engaged with all aspects of this city, its light and its dark, a city that couldn't decide if it wished to embrace its past or be rid of it once and for all.

It was Sofia who introduced me to the mayor, and she who extracted from him a firm promise that one day my Lviv—the city of law students, professors and grandfathers—would be properly commemorated. Here in *Trapezna*, deep below the Bernardine, was where we liked to sit and talk. Sofia and her partner Andrei, he of the fine photographic eye, and their friend Iris, who had devoted years to the well-being of the city's many endangered buildings, along with her partner Ben, the only British person I ever came across in Lviv. Here we sat and wondered about the city and the country as they went through new traumas, inevitably connected to past events. Here we could talk about nationalists and nationalism, about the men who brought antique guns and yellow-and-blue flags to the piazza opposite the Opera House. We could talk of east and west, of the pull to Europe and hoped-for modernity, of the push to Russia and fault lines, of a Malaysian plane shot from the sky a thousand kilometres to the east, of demonstrations and killings on Kiev's Maidan Square, of the annexation of Crimea, of corruption past and present, of Ukrainian presidents then and now, of lectures and talks delivered in the University's Hall of Mirrors, of our plans to celebrate the city.

The city was Sofia's life. From a high-ceilinged Secession building on Akademika Bohomol'tsya Street (ul. Asnyka) she and her colleagues worked on publications, exhibitions, research and lectures, and the truly outstanding website on which were gathered maps of the city dating from 1635 to the present day. They added countless images and accounts and testimonies, idyllic and not so idyllic. In this virtual place you could traverse the entirety of the city, across time and space.

One of Sofia's projects was the restoration of the sad remains of the Golden Rose Synagogue, on Blacharska Street (now Ivana Fedorova Street). The original stone structure was said to have been saved from seventeenth-century oblivion by Róża Nachmanowicz, the daughter-in-law of its founder, a tale recorded in a theatrical piece written by Józef Wittlin, who was also a playwright. I tried to find the pages, without success. The Nazis did for the building, three centuries later, as they did for its worshippers. Now it was a ruin, what remained of its dignity hidden behind a protective metal fence. The best view—the only view—was from the terrace of the *Golden Rose* restaurant, surely the most dire establishment in the entire city, a Jewish-themed restaurant where patrons were encouraged to wear black hats and other paraphernalia of Orthodox Jewry, invited to eat pork sausages and haggle over the price of a meal at an establishment whose menu has no prices (I never was able to get to the bottom of the city's penchant for themed eateries: there was *Kryjivka*, a basement bar that honoured the Ukrainian Insurgent Army that battled the Red Army in World War II; *Café Masoch*, which celebrated Lviv-born writer Leopold von Sacher-Masoch, a place where leather-clad waitresses were willing to chain you to a chair and engage in minor whipping; and the idea for a restaurant that celebrates the life of the dwarf, one that didn't come to fruition in the face of insurmountable opposition).

The terrace at the *Golden Rose* was now gone, a consequence of the efforts of Sofia, Iris and various public officials to mark the site, a project of the Lviv City Council and the German Government, despite opposition from a curious coalition that included the ultra-nationalists and the ultra-religious, as well as an irate restaurant owner. The planned memorial was set to include a series of stones on which would be engraved the recollections of former residents. When Sofia asked who I might want to include, I suggested Inka Katz, the niece of Hersch Lauterpacht, who was fourteen years old when the Germans took the city in the summer of 1941, the only member of her extended Lvovian family to survive the decimation. I once drank black tea with Inka in her light-filled apartment in Paris' sixteenth arrondissement, near the Eiffel Tower. She recalled—as though it were yesterday—the last sight she ever had of her parents, on Sykstuska Street, a scene she observed from on high, looking down from a window of their small apartment, as they were arrested by Germans and the Ukrainian Auxiliary Police:

> "my mother had been taken... I saw everything looking out of the window. I was twelve. I wasn't a child any more. I stopped being a child in 1939... I saw my father running after my mother, behind her, on the street. I understood, it was over. I knew what was happening. I can still visualize the scene, my mother's dress, her high heels..."

Inka took refuge, first with a Polish governess, then with other acquaintances, finally in a small convent somewhere in the city, a place and a name she could no longer recall.

Sitting with her in Paris, we talked of Wittlin and his novel *Salt of the Earth*, of the power of imagination, of harmony reigning among those who professed different faiths and views.

"Let's play at idylls. Let's just play games and close our eyes."

VIII

A couple of summers ago I spent a few days in Lviv with Niklas Frank, the son of Hans, and Horst von Wächter, the son of Otto. The two men, who were born just a few weeks apart in 1939, spent a part of their early years with their Governor fathers in Nazi-occupied Poland. I had come to know them whilst researching my book on my grandfather's early life, and on the city's connection with the origins of "genocide" and "crimes against humanity".

Between 1939 and 1945 the two Governors were responsible for actions that led to the deaths of millions of Jews and Poles, yet the two sons had sharply different attitudes to their fathers. Niklas considered his father to be a criminal: "I am against the death penalty," he once told me, "but not in the case of my father." Horst wanted to love his father and saw him as an essentially decent man who happened to be part of a bad system: "I see things different," he explained, "from the first moment in Lemberg... he actually tried to do something positive."

We came together to the city to make a documentary (*My Nazi Legacy*). We stood on a city hill admiring the vista. We visited the house where Horst lived as a child, now a children's home. We talked about responsibility in the splendid debating chamber of the former Galician Parliament of the Austro-Hungarian Empire, the room in which Hans Frank announced the extermination of all the city's Jews in the presence of Otto von Wächter. Niklas surprised us when he climbed onto the stage, pulled a sheet of paper from his back pocket and read out an extract of the speech his father had given from the same spot, noting his father's abundant sense of humour:

> "Party Comrade Wächter, I have to say this: you did well! In a year's time you have made forgotten what a filthy dump this was. Lemberg is once again a true and proud German city. I do not speak about the Jews that we still have here. We will deal with them, of course. By the way, I hardly saw any of them today. What has happened? I was told that this city used to swarm with thousands and thousands of these flat-footed Indians—but I could see none. You have not done anything nasty to them, have you?"

Niklas paused, to point out that the Protokol reported the reaction in the audience: "Great hilarity".

Later the three of us visited the City Archives to look at documents. Horst signed the visitor's book, and I noticed that after his name he added: "Son of the Governor". The next day we drove to nearby Zhovkva. First we visited the remains of the seventeenth-century synagogue. In the afternoon, in stifling heat, we visited the birch and oak wood where 3,500 bodies lay. "This our fathers did," Niklas said imploringly to Horst, who plucked the petals off a small white flower and spoke of his grandfather's war on this land a century earlier.

Our road trip ended the next day near Chervone, about forty kilometres from Lviv, on the way to the town of Brody, where Joseph Roth was born. On a lovely, warm July day we observed on a hill the bright white headstones in neat rows that marked the graves of the fallen, set against the bright grass. In one corner of the field fresh graves were being dug. "To hold the mortal remains of Germans and Ukrainians who died fighting the Soviet Red Army in the summer of 1944", we were told. The soldiers' bodies were recently discovered by farmers, as they ploughed. The sound of metal on earth was accompanied by the unexpected and beautiful lament of a small choir and orchestra, with a prominent double bass.

Several hundred people were gathered here, at the annual celebration of the Waffen SS Galizien Division created by Horst's father in 1943. This was the first such SS division to involve non-Germans, Ukrainians who volunteered in large numbers to fight the hated Red Army on the approaching Eastern Front. Those gathered included a smattering of elderly World War II veterans, old men with walking sticks, medals and ribbons. There were locals—families with children—and some sympathizers associated with the extreme Ukraine nationalist party, *Svoboda* (Freedom). We were treated with polite curiosity. No one objected to our presence, or to the camera crew.

At a certain point during the afternoon the camera fixed on Horst in conversation with a man who called himself Wolf Sturm. It wasn't the oversized leather boots or the dark glasses, or even the machine-gun slung over his shoulder that was so shocking. It was the uniform, worn with obvious pride: Wolf wore the well-pressed and familiar (from World War II movies) grey uniform of the Waffen SS, complete with Death's Heads, swastikas and a Ukrainian lion. And he was not alone: several other men formed a little group of smiling, comfortable, modern Nazis. Niklas was horrified, but Horst was uninhibited enough to allow us to see for ourselves how comfortable he was in surroundings that recalled—and celebrated—another age.

We drove back to Lviv in silence.

IX

The street on which Wittlin had his many homes, Abbot Hoffman Street (Chekhova Street), is only a short distance from Sofia's office, in the old Łyczaków district. The two places were connected by residential backstreets, on which you will no longer find horse-drawn cabs or tenements with obvious caretakers, although you might pass a swastika recently daubed on a pink wall. The smell of camphor lingered no more, Abbot Hoffman had lost its harlots and chimney sweeps, its cobblers and grocers, its Poles and Jews. They and the others were washed away by the tides of history. You could get a sense of what had been lost from the writings of Mykhailo Yatskiv, essayist and purveyor of miniature stories that touched on the darker elements of street life. He too now resided in the grounds of the nearby Lychakiv cemetery.

As with so many parts of this architecturally preserved city, the residents were swept away en masse even as their homes remained intact. The buildings were as they were back then, some with front doors still ajar. Into these build-ings you could wander, the places where Wittlin lived. If you started on the eastern side, between number 3 and number 9, on the wall of number 7, you could look into the large bronze eyes of Joseph Roth. He stared out across the street from the wall of his uncle's house, on a plaque that recorded his visits. The celebrated essayist was remembered not as a Jew or Pole but as an "Austrian writer". It seemed that the struggle over identities was never-ending.

Cross the street and enter number 30, tucked between two small shops. Walk into the gloom, head left, on the small

black-and-white tiled floor, then up the wooden stairwell with its metal banister and deep blue wall. If you stood on the half landing, looked out of the window, listened and smelled, peered into the empty yard, you could forget that a hundred years had passed. Was it any different at number 20, or at number 6, or over the road at No. 2 Bonifratry Street (Akademika Mykhaila Kravchuka Street)?

This was my Lviv. The city of Leon, of Lauterpacht and Lemkin, stuck in the early years of the twentieth century. I too could imagine a final procession, one led by my three guides, to which I would invite all my new Ukrainian friends. Together we would head off from Abbot Hoffman Street, alive to the sound of the *Lemberg Waltz* being beaten out on Leopold Kozłowski's old piano, towards the Union Hill on a final dance across the city.

Along Łyczakowska Street we would waltz, onto the Bernardyński Square and past the pharmacy once known as the old "Hungarian Crown", the one with "the most beautiful shop window in all Galicia and Lodomeria", on the windowpanes of which were etched the garlands and Secession water lilies and the exquisite crown of St Stephen. Onward, past the column that bore the stone image of Adam Mickiewicz, standing near the George Hotel. Then to Teatralna, a place of pilgrimage for anyone with an interest in the rule of law and modern human rights, Hersch Lauterpacht's street during his Lemberg years. On we would waltz, past the entrance to the bookstore above which was

carved the street's old Polish name—ul. Rutowskiego—set in stone in honour of Dr Tadeusz Rutowski, President of the city, he of mild deafness, taken hostage by the departing Russians after the occupation of September 1914. Here I might pause, to invite my friends to look towards St George's Cathedral and the house where Leon was born, to join me in taking in the moment, to partake in the act of recognizance, of how the spirit of the city had infused Leon and then been passed on to me in that most mysterious of ways, not having been the subject of a single conversation between us.

Along Teatralna our dance might continue, with an added spring, out of sight of the Opera House, to number 6 and the grey stone building—now a Cossack Hostel—where Lauterpacht lived as a student, the place to which he returned every day over eight semesters, through iron doors marked at their centre with a large iron "L". Lauterpacht? Lemberg? Lwów? Lviv? On we went, past number 10, under the balcony, into the covered alley that connects Teatralna to the Market Square and the Town Hall, towards the *Na Bambetli* coffee shop with its collection of fine teas, past the wall on which the plaster had been cut away to reveal the red and black words of an old Polish advertisement: *OBUWIE*, it proclaimed, the remnant of a shop at which Lemkin might have bought a hat, or perhaps a pair of shoes, an establishment now remembered with a fine swastika, this one offered in blue.

Into the main square we could proceed, in sight of the Town Hall and a myriad other details that distracted us from that which we do not wish to see. Look carefully at the mighty door frames. Look for the empty niches carved into the old stone, in which there once nestled the tiny pieces of parchment with a verse from the Torah. Look for number 14, from above which the winged lion still looks down, resting on the pages of a book that remains open on words forever unfulfilled. "PAX TIBI MARCE EVANGELISTA MEUS", the lion proclaims, "Peace to you, Mark, my evangelist!" Once the home of the ambassador of Venice to the city, the odours of stagnant water, fish, wine, olive oil and wisteria were gone, replaced by the sweet scent of fresh strudel.

Into the north side of the square our waltz continues, past the *Atlas* Café, onto Drukars'ka Street where we can stop and admire the stencilled image of AH, the force of his famous face replaced with the power of words: "Lemberg Macht Frei". From here it is upward to the heavens, to the highest point in the city, to Castle Hill, known once as the Union of Lublin Mound. Here our dance will end, as we look out over the city at dusk, alive to each single bulb as it flickers on. Look down towards Miodowa Street, by no means as sweet as honey.

On our way along the trails that lead to the upper terrace, we might pass others who would be following the bareheaded steps of Józef Wittlin and other members of his "Idiots' Club". Some would linger, among them a young

Arthur Goodhart, the lawyer who visited the city in the summer of 1919, a member of the commission charged by President Woodrow Wilson to report on the protection of minority groups in Poland. Goodhart climbed the hill with Dr Tadeusz Fiedler, President of the Lwów Polytechnic, two men wondering what might be done to reduce the tensions between the various communities. Could new laws help? With so mixed a population, Dr Fiedler told Mr Goodhart, the solution would not be so simple.

At the top of the hill, our dance would finally end. As the piano fell silent, we would be joined by Lauterpacht and Lemkin, long forgotten in this city, two men who it seems never actually met, not in Lviv or anywhere else. As true Lvovians they would surely have aired their differences, and done so with passion and energy.

"We must focus on the protection of the individual," I would hear Lauterpacht insist, "irrespective of which group they happen to be a member of."

"No, no, no," Lemkin shouts back, with ferocious passion, "our focus must be on the protection of cultures in all their diversity, and to do that we must protect the groups."

"Why do you insist so?" Lauterpacht says quietly.

"People here were mistreated because they were members of a group," Lemkin responds, "not because of their individual qualities."

"That may be true," Lauterpacht retorts, "but it is also true that the word you have invented will elevate the group and undermine the protection of individuals. You are replacing the tyranny of the sovereign with the tyranny of the group."

On they go, over time and place, across the world and its courtrooms.

Leon and I would watch on, in silence and in awe.

This was our Lviv. Not quiet or pure, but everywhere.

Hampstead, London, May 2016.

LIST OF ILLUSTRATIONS

PHOTOGRAPHS BY DIANA MATAR

MAZEL TOV
J.S. MARGOT

DAYS IN THE CAUCASUS
BANINE

ON LOVE AND TYRANNY
ANN HEBERLEIN

THOSE WHO FORGET
GÉRALDINE SCHWARZ

YOUNG REMBRANDT
ONNO BLOM

THE WORLD OF YESTERDAY
STEFAN ZWEIG

NO PLACE TO LAY ONE'S HEAD
FRANÇOISE FRENKEL

DREAMERS
VOLKER WEIDERMANN

THE LIMITS OF MY LANGUAGE
EVA MEIJER

A CHILL IN THE AIR
IRIS ORIGO

RED LOVE
MAXIM LEO

A WORLD GONE MAD
ASTRID LINDGREN

ON THE END OF THE WORLD
JOSEPH ROTH

SORROW OF THE EARTH
ERIC VUILLARD

A SORROW BEYOND DREAMS
PETER HANDKE

MEMORIES: FROM MOSCOW TO THE BLACK SEA
TEFFI